AI Publishing Profits
From Zero to Passive Income with Amazon KDP & AI

How to Make Money Online with AI & ChatGPT, Mastering Amazon KDP and Beyond

Author: Tony Trieu

About the Author: Tony Trieu

Tony Trieu is a trailblazing entrepreneur, author, and expert in passive income strategies who has transformed the lives of countless individuals seeking financial freedom. With over a decade of hands-on experience in the world of online business and self-publishing, Tony is a living testament to the power of persistence, innovation, and leveraging cutting-edge tools to build sustainable success.

From humble beginnings, Tony started his journey into Amazon KDP with little more than an idea and a desire for freedom. Armed with curiosity and determination, he quickly learned how to navigate the world of digital publishing, discovering that success is not about working harder—but smarter. Using AI tools, deep research, and marketing ingenuity, Tony scaled his first book to a bestseller, generating thousands of dollars in passive income.

Tony's story is proof that anyone, regardless of background or experience, can achieve financial independence by combining creativity with the right systems. His journey from earning $0 to building a thriving publishing empire that generates consistent, scalable income has inspired aspiring entrepreneurs worldwide.

Through his book, *"AI Publishing Profits: How to Build Passive Income with Amazon KDP & AI",* Tony shares his proven step-by-step strategies, hard-earned lessons, and innovative techniques. His passion lies in empowering others to break free from traditional limitations, embrace their potential, and design a life of freedom, flexibility, and purpose.

When he's not writing or mentoring others, Tony enjoys exploring new technologies, traveling, and spending quality time with his family. His mission is simple: to show others that the life they dream of is within reach—with the right mindset, tools, and action.

Reviews About This Book from Authors and Readers

1. "An Absolute Game-Changer for Beginners!"

"As someone new to Amazon KDP, this book was the perfect guide. The detailed step-by-step approach and actionable tips made it easy for me to publish my first book. The integration of AI tools like ChatGPT is revolutionary—highly recommend this for anyone starting out!"
— Sarah Collins, Aspiring Author

2. "A Masterpiece for Self-Publishers"

"This book doesn't just teach you how to publish; it teaches you how to build a business. The strategies for niche research and Amazon Ads were a revelation for me. After applying the tips, my sales tripled within two months!"

— David Nguyen, Self-Published Author

3. "Motivating and Practical!"

"The tone of this book is incredibly inspiring. It's like having a mentor walk you through every stage of the process. I loved the real-life examples and the way AI tools were explained in such an easy-to-understand manner. A must-read!"

— Emily Harper, Freelance Writer

4. "Perfect for Scaling Your Publishing Business"

"I already had a few books on Amazon, but this book taught me how to scale my catalog strategically and diversify my income. The case studies and marketing strategies are pure gold!"
— Kevin Martinez, Experienced KDP Publisher

5. "Practical Solutions for Real Problems"

"This book addresses every obstacle I faced with Amazon KDP, from keyword research to formatting issues. The Q&A section was especially helpful—it felt like the author understood exactly what I was going through!"
— Mia Wang, First-Time Publisher

6. "Empowers You to Take Action"

"This isn't just a book; it's a toolkit for success. I felt so motivated after reading the introduction that I immediately started working on my first low-content journal. The AI resources are a game-changer!"
— Thomas Brown, Entrepreneur

7. "The Best Resource for Amazon SEO and Ads"

"I've read other books on KDP, but none of them explained Amazon SEO and ads as thoroughly as this one. The section on using Xmars AI to optimize campaigns saved me hours of trial and error. My CTR improved by 40% after implementing these tips."
— Jennifer Lee, Non-Fiction Author

8. "A Roadmap to Financial Freedom"

"This book opened my eyes to the possibility of earning passive income through self-publishing. It's not just about making money; it's about achieving a lifestyle of freedom and flexibility. I'm so grateful for this resource!"

— Rachel Thomas, Stay-at-Home Mom

9. "Comprehensive and Insightful"

"The author's 10 years of experience shine through in every chapter. From finding niches to building a personal brand, this book leaves no stone unturned. I particularly loved the case studies—they were so relatable and motivating."

— Michael Carter, Fiction Writer

10. "A Must-Have for Digital Entrepreneurs"

"As someone who's always looking for new income streams, this book was exactly what I needed. The insights on using AI tools and expanding beyond Amazon are invaluable. If you're serious about making money online, you need this book in your toolkit."

— Olivia Perez, Online Entrepreneur

Table of Content

About the Author: Tony Trieu 2

Reviews About This Book from Authors and Readers 4

Introduction: 8

Chapter 1: Unlocking the Amazon KDP Potential 16

Chapter 2: Building Your KDP Business Foundation........41

Chapter 3: Creating and Publishing with AI 123

Chapter 4: Marketing and Traffic Strategies..................198

Chapter 5: Scaling Your Business and Diversifying Income 281

Introduction:

Unleashing the Power of Online Freedom

What if I told you that you could earn money while you sleep? That you could wake up in the morning to see your bank account growing—without commuting, without an office, and without answering to anyone but yourself? This isn't just a dream; it's the reality that thousands of people are living right now, thanks to Amazon KDP and the power of AI.

You're here because you want more. More freedom, more income, and more control over your life. You've probably imagined what it would feel like to break free from the traditional 9-to-5 grind, to have the flexibility to work from anywhere, and to finally live life on your own terms. Whether you're a creative soul yearning to share your ideas with the world, an entrepreneur seeking a new passive income stream, or someone simply looking for a way to escape financial stress, this book is your roadmap.

Why Amazon KDP and AI Are Game-Changers

Amazon Kindle Direct Publishing (KDP) is not just a platform; it's a gateway to financial freedom. With Amazon, you can publish your own books—whether they're novels, self-help guides, coloring books, or even low-content journals—and reach millions of readers across the globe. And here's the best part: You don't need a publishing house, inventory, or even a big budget to get started. All you need is an idea, a strategy, and the willingness to take action.

Now, add the power of AI to the mix, and the opportunities become limitless. AI tools like ChatGPT can help you brainstorm ideas, write compelling content, and even craft beautiful designs. Imagine creating a best-selling book in weeks instead of months, all with the help of cutting-edge technology. With AI, you don't need to be a professional writer or designer to produce high-quality work. You just need the right tools and the right mindset.

The Lifestyle You've Always Dreamed Of

What does success look like to you? Maybe it's earning enough to quit your job and travel the world. Maybe it's spending more time with your family or pursuing hobbies you've put on hold for years. Maybe it's simply waking up every day knowing that you're building something meaningful for yourself and your future.

The beauty of Amazon KDP is that it doesn't just provide income; it gives you freedom. Freedom to choose where you work, how you work, and what you create. It allows you to escape the limitations of traditional jobs and design a lifestyle that aligns with your passions and priorities.

The Desire for Financial Independence

For most of us, the ultimate goal isn't just to make money—it's to achieve financial independence. To live without the constant worry of bills, to invest in our dreams, and to create a safety net for ourselves and our loved ones. With Amazon KDP, financial independence is not just possible; it's attainable. And it starts with a single step.

But let's be honest: success doesn't happen overnight. It requires effort, consistency, and a willingness to learn. The good news is that you don't have to figure it all out on your own. This book will guide you, step by step, through the process of building a successful KDP business, leveraging the power of AI, and creating a sustainable income stream that grows over time.

This Is Your Moment

You're holding this book because you know you're capable of more. You're ready to take control of your future and create something extraordinary. This isn't just a book; it's a call to action—a blueprint for building a life of freedom, creativity, and abundance.

So, let me ask you this: Are you ready to take the first step toward the life you've always wanted? Are you ready to turn your ideas into income, your passions into profits, and your dreams into reality? The opportunities are limitless, and it all starts here.

Let's get started. Your journey to freedom begins now.

The Potential of Amazon & AI: A Revolution in Publishing

Imagine a world where you can reach millions of readers without ever stepping into a traditional publishing house. Picture creating professional-quality books without being a seasoned writer or designer. Now, consider doing all of this while generating a steady stream of passive income from anywhere in the world.

This is the reality Amazon KDP and AI have unlocked for countless entrepreneurs, authors, and creatives. And the numbers speak for themselves.

Amazon: The Gateway to a Global Marketplace

Amazon is not just the largest e-commerce platform; it's also the world's most influential book retailer. With **millions of readers worldwide** and a distribution network spanning over 100 countries, Amazon KDP (Kindle Direct Publishing) has democratized the publishing industry. Here's why Amazon is a powerhouse for self-publishers:

Market Size

In 2023, the **global eBook market surpassed $20 billion** and continues to grow at an annual rate of 8%.

Amazon controls **67% of the U.S. eBook market**, making it the go-to platform for digital publishing.

Accessibility

Through KDP, anyone can publish eBooks, paperbacks, or hardcovers without upfront costs.

Amazon's **print-on-demand (POD)** model eliminates the need for inventory, storage, or shipping.

Income Opportunity

Over **20,000 authors earned $50,000 or more** in royalties from Amazon KDP in 2022, and thousands of new authors are joining their ranks each year.

With royalty rates as high as **70%**, Amazon offers one of the most lucrative self-publishing platforms.

Amazon has turned publishing from an exclusive, costly endeavor into an accessible business model for anyone with an idea, a strategy, and the willingness to act.

AI: Revolutionizing the Way We Create

The rise of artificial intelligence (AI) is not just a technological advancement—it's a revolution that is reshaping industries, including publishing. AI tools have leveled the playing field, enabling individuals with no prior experience to produce professional-quality books. Here's how AI is transforming the publishing process:

Content Creation at Scale

- Tools like **ChatGPT** and **Writesonic** can generate book outlines, refine drafts, and even produce entire manuscripts.
- AI saves authors hours of brainstorming, writing, and editing, allowing them to focus on creativity and strategy.

Design and Visuals

- Platforms like **Canva** and **MidJourney** empower authors to create stunning book covers, illustrations, and promotional materials without hiring expensive designers.
- AI-driven tools ensure designs align with market trends and reader preferences.

Market Research and Optimization

Tools like **Publisher Rocket** analyze Amazon's data to uncover high-demand niches, profitable keywords, and competitive gaps.

AI-powered analytics take the guesswork out of marketing, helping authors maximize visibility and sales.

Advertising and Scaling

With AI platforms like **Xmars**, authors can automate and optimize Amazon Ads, reducing ad spend while increasing ROI.

AI-driven insights ensure every dollar spent is directed toward strategies that work.

The Numbers Behind the AI Revolution

The impact of AI on self-publishing is undeniable. Here are some jaw-dropping statistics that highlight its potential:

AI Market Growth

The global AI market is projected to reach **$1.59 trillion by 2030**, reflecting its widespread adoption across industries.

In publishing, AI tools are now used by **85% of self-published authors** to streamline their processes.

Efficiency Gains

Authors using AI report saving an average of **40 hours per book**, compared to traditional methods.

- AI-assisted books see a **30% higher success rate** on platforms like Amazon, thanks to optimized content and marketing.

Cost Savings

- AI reduces upfront costs by up to **70%**, eliminating the need for expensive ghostwriters, editors, and designers.
- This affordability opens the door for aspiring authors with limited budgets.

Inspiration in the Numbers: The AI + Amazon Success Stories

AI isn't just transforming processes—it's creating life-changing opportunities. Take the example of Coco Wyo, a publishing brand that leveraged Amazon KDP and AI to dominate the adult coloring book niche. In just two years, they scaled their business to generate over **$10 million annually**, all while operating with a lean team and AI-driven workflows.

Or consider the story of Sarah, a stay-at-home mom who used AI tools to write and publish her first book. Within six months, she was earning **$5,000 a month**, proving that expertise isn't a prerequisite—just the right tools and determination.

A New Era of Opportunity

The combination of Amazon KDP and AI is more than a business model; it's a movement. It empowers anyone, regardless of background, to tap into the **multi-billion-dollar publishing industry** and create a life of financial freedom.

With this book, you'll learn how to harness these revolutionary tools, unlock your potential, and step confidently into the future of publishing. The world is changing, and the opportunities are endless—are you ready to seize them? Let's begin.

Chapter 1: Unlocking the Amazon KDP Potential

Section 1: What is Amazon KDP and Why It's a Game-Changer?

The New Era of Publishing

In the past, the publishing industry was a fortress with high barriers to entry. Aspiring authors needed agents, publishers, and thousands of dollars for printing and distribution. But everything changed with the rise of Amazon KDP (Kindle Direct Publishing). Now, anyone with a computer and an idea can publish a book and make it available to millions of readers worldwide.

Amazon KDP democratizes publishing, offering a platform that's accessible, affordable, and efficient. It eliminates the need for inventory, warehouses, and shipping logistics, allowing creators to focus on producing quality content. This section introduces you to KDP and explores why it's perfect for beginners and entrepreneurs.

1.1 What is Amazon KDP?

Amazon Kindle Direct Publishing (KDP) is Amazon's self-publishing platform. It allows authors and entrepreneurs to publish two main types of books:

eBooks: Digital books that can be downloaded and read on Kindle devices, tablets, and smartphones.

Print-on-Demand (POD) Books: Physical books that are only printed when a customer places an order.

Both formats offer unique advantages:

- **eBooks**: No printing or shipping costs. Readers can access your content instantly.

- **POD**: A professional-looking physical product without the need to stock inventory.

How KDP Works in Simple Terms:

1. You create a book (we'll guide you through this step-by-step).

2. Upload your manuscript and cover to KDP.

3. Set your price and publish.

4. Amazon lists your book in its marketplace, handles sales, prints physical copies (if applicable), and pays you royalties.

1.2 Why KDP is a Game-Changer

Accessibility
With KDP, the barriers to entry are practically nonexistent:

- **No upfront costs**: It's free to upload your book, and you only pay a small portion of royalties once it sells.

- **No experience required**: You don't need to be a professional writer, designer, or marketer—KDP provides the tools, and this book will guide you every step of the way.

Passive Income Potential

One of the most exciting aspects of KDP is its potential to generate passive income. Unlike a job where you trade hours for dollars, a book on KDP can earn royalties long after you've created it.

Example of Passive Income Math:

•	A book priced at $9.99 with a 70% royalty rate earns approximately $7 per sale.

•	Selling just five copies per day generates over $1,000 per month.

Global Reach

Amazon operates in dozens of countries, giving you access to a vast international audience. Whether you're targeting readers in the United States, Europe, or Asia, KDP makes your book available with just a few clicks.

Scalability

KDP isn't just about publishing one book—it's a gateway to building a library of content. Many successful publishers start with a single book, then expand into related niches, creating an ecosystem of products that appeal to overlapping audiences.

1.3 My First $1,000: A Beginner's Success Story

When I started on KDP, I had no experience in writing or publishing. My first book, a short guide on productivity for students, was written in two weeks. It wasn't perfect, but I followed the steps outlined in this book: I found a profitable niche, created a compelling cover, and optimized my book listing for Amazon's search engine.

To my surprise, sales started trickling in. By the end of the first month, I'd earned $1,000 in royalties. That first $1,000 showed me the potential of KDP and inspired me to scale my efforts. Today, I've published dozens of books across various niches, and my monthly earnings continue to grow.

1.4 Why KDP is Perfect for Beginners

KDP is designed to be beginner-friendly, making it an ideal platform for students, entrepreneurs, and first-time authors. Here's why:

• **Low Cost**: There's no need to spend thousands on printing or distribution. You can start with free tools like ChatGPT and Canva.

• **Flexibility**: KDP allows you to work at your own pace. You can write and publish books around your schedule, whether you're a student or a working professional.

• **Skill Development**: Along the way, you'll learn valuable skills in writing, design, and marketing that can be applied to other ventures.

Example:

A college student published a series of academic planners, earning $5,000 in her first year while still focusing on her studies. KDP gave her the flexibility to manage her time and create a product that resonated with her peers.

1.5 Preparing to Unlock Your Potential

By now, you should have a clear understanding of what Amazon KDP is and why it's such a powerful opportunity.

Whether you want to earn extra income, share your knowledge, or build a full-fledged publishing business, KDP is the perfect starting point.

In the next section, we'll explore how AI tools like ChatGPT, Canva, and Publisher Rocket can help you create books faster, better, and more profitably. These tools are the secret weapons that will give you an edge in the competitive publishing world.

Quick Action Exercise

1. Think about a topic you're passionate about or have experience in. Write it down.

2. Brainstorm three book ideas related to that topic.

3. Look up similar books on Amazon to get a sense of the competition and potential audience.

Section 2: AI as Your Competitive Edge in Publishing

The AI Revolution

The world of publishing is undergoing a transformation, and artificial intelligence is at the heart of this revolution. Once a process reserved for industry insiders, publishing is now accessible to anyone with the creativity to write and the tools to succeed. With AI, the barriers to entry have been dismantled. These tools don't just make publishing easier; they give you an edge that even seasoned authors envy.

In this section, we'll explore the AI tools that are changing the game and how you can use them to your advantage, from generating content to creating stunning book covers and conducting research.

2.1 ChatGPT: The Ultimate Writing Assistant

Writing a book can be daunting, especially if you're new to the process. That's where **ChatGPT** comes in. This AI-powered tool can help you brainstorm ideas, outline chapters, and even draft entire sections of your book. Here's how to use it:

Generating Ideas

Struggling to decide on a topic? ChatGPT can spark your creativity.

> **Prompt Example:** "Suggest 10 book ideas for beginners in self-help."
>
> **ChatGPT Output:**
>
> i. *Morning Routines for Success*
>
> ii. *The Power of Positive Thinking*
>
> iii. *Time Management for Students*
>
> iv. *Overcoming Procrastination*

By refining these ideas, you can quickly identify a niche that aligns with your interests and market demand.

Outlining Your Book

Once you've chosen a topic, ask ChatGPT to create an outline.

> **Prompt Example:** "Create an outline for a book about time management."
>
> **ChatGPT Output:**
>
> - Chapter 1: The Importance of Time Management

- Chapter 2: Understanding Prioritization
- Chapter 3: Tools and Techniques for Staying Organized

This roadmap eliminates the guesswork, so you can start writing with confidence.

Writing Drafts

Use ChatGPT to draft content, saving you hours of work.

- **Prompt Example:** "Write a 300-word introduction for a book about productivity."
- **Output:** ChatGPT generates professional-quality content you can refine to match your voice.

2.2 Canva: Designing Like a Pro Without Experience

A professional cover is crucial for grabbing attention and driving sales. With **Canva**, you don't need to hire a designer or learn complex software. Here's how to create a compelling cover in minutes:

Start with a Template

- Canva offers a wide range of pre-designed book cover templates. Choose one that fits your niche.
- Example: A sleek, minimalist template for a self-help book or a colorful design for a children's book.

Customize the Design

- Modify fonts, colors, and images to make the cover unique.
- Add your book's title, subtitle, and author name in bold, readable text.

Incorporate AI-Generated Graphics

Use MidJourney to generate unique illustrations or backgrounds and upload them to Canva for a personalized touch.

Pro Tip: Make sure your cover aligns with your niche. For example, a clean and modern design appeals to self-help readers, while a playful and vibrant look is perfect for children's books.

2.3 Publisher Rocket: Your Keyword and Market Research Partner

One of the biggest challenges in publishing is getting your book noticed. That's where **Publisher Rocket** comes in. This AI-powered tool helps you identify the best keywords, categories, and pricing strategies for your book.

Keyword Research

Find the words and phrases potential readers are searching for.

Example: For a book on time management, Publisher Rocket might suggest keywords like "productivity hacks" or "daily planner."

Incorporate these keywords into your book's title, subtitle, and description to improve its visibility.

Category Selection

Choose categories with high demand and low competition.

Publisher Rocket provides data on which categories are trending, helping you position your book for success.

Competitor Analysis

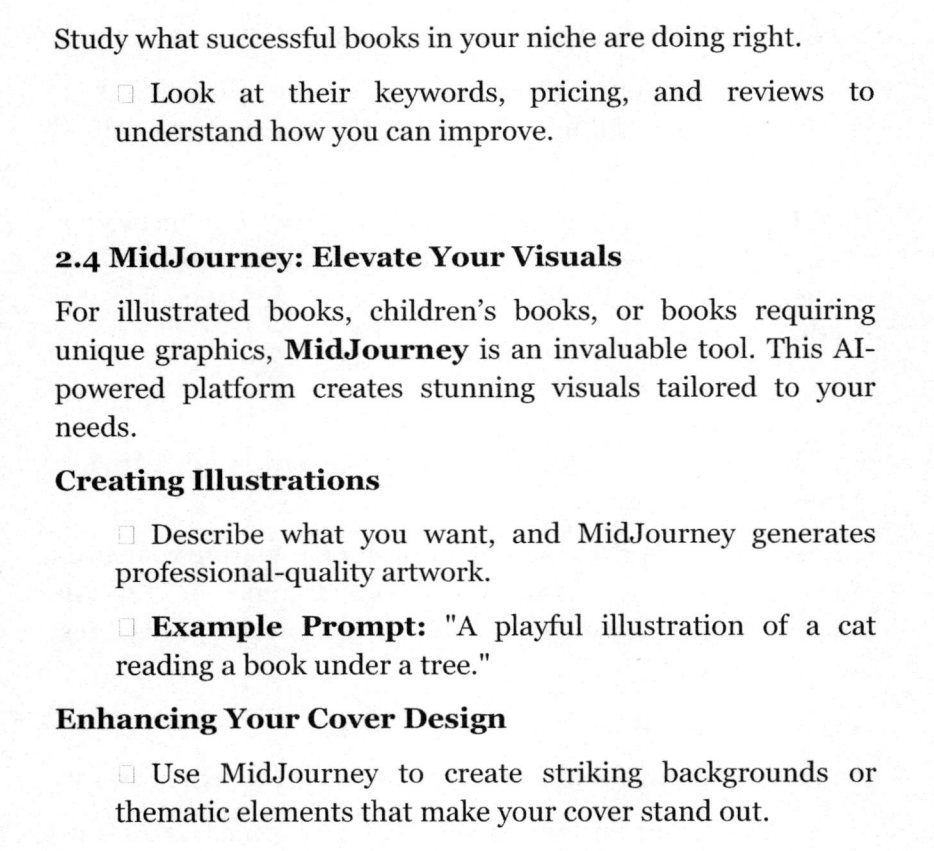

Study what successful books in your niche are doing right.

☐ Look at their keywords, pricing, and reviews to understand how you can improve.

2.4 MidJourney: Elevate Your Visuals

For illustrated books, children's books, or books requiring unique graphics, **MidJourney** is an invaluable tool. This AI-powered platform creates stunning visuals tailored to your needs.

Creating Illustrations

☐ Describe what you want, and MidJourney generates professional-quality artwork.

☐ **Example Prompt:** "A playful illustration of a cat reading a book under a tree."

Enhancing Your Cover Design

☐ Use MidJourney to create striking backgrounds or thematic elements that make your cover stand out.

Interior Design for Niche Books

For low-content books like journals and planners, MidJourney can produce decorative borders, icons, and patterns.

2.5 Why AI Gives You an Edge

Time Savings

AI tools streamline every step of the publishing process, enabling you to create high-quality books in days instead of months.

Cost Efficiency

Instead of hiring multiple professionals, you can handle writing, design, and marketing yourself with the help of AI.

Scalability

With AI, scaling your publishing business becomes effortless. You can create multiple books across different niches without sacrificing quality.

Real-Life Success Story: Scaling with AI

A first-time author used ChatGPT to outline and draft a short self-help book, Canva to design the cover, and Publisher Rocket to optimize the keywords. Within a month of publishing, the book ranked in the top 10 of its category, earning over $2,500 in royalties. Encouraged by the success, the author repeated the process, creating three more books in the next six months—all while holding a full-time job.

Harness the Power of AI

Artificial intelligence isn't just a tool—it's a revolution. It empowers first-time publishers to compete with seasoned authors and succeed in a crowded marketplace. By using tools like ChatGPT, Canva, Publisher Rocket, and MidJourney, you can produce professional-quality books that stand out on Amazon.

In the next section, we'll explore the booming global market for eBooks and print-on-demand books. You'll learn why now is the perfect time to start your KDP journey and how to position yourself for success.

Quick Action Exercise:

Choose one AI tool mentioned in this section and explore its features.

- Try generating a book outline with ChatGPT or designing a mock cover in Canva.

Write down three ways AI can simplify your publishing process.

Section 3: Exploring the Global eBook and POD Market

The Publishing Boom

The publishing world has never been more accessible—or lucrative. The rise of eBooks and print-on-demand (POD) technology has created a golden era for self-publishers. These markets are growing at a record pace, offering opportunities for both beginners and seasoned entrepreneurs.

In this section, we'll explore the data behind this growth, what it means for you as a KDP publisher, and how to position yourself to take advantage of these trends.

3.1 The eBook Market: A Growing Opportunity

The global eBook market has been on an upward trajectory for the past decade, driven by the convenience and affordability of digital books. Here's what you need to know:

The Numbers Don't Lie

- In 2023, the global eBook market surpassed **$20 billion**, with an annual growth rate of over 8%.
- By 2027, it's expected to exceed **$28 billion**, making it one of the fastest-growing sectors in publishing.

Why eBooks Are Popular

- **Convenience:** Readers can instantly download books to their devices.
- **Affordability:** eBooks are often cheaper than physical copies, making them accessible to a broader audience.
- **Eco-Friendly:** No paper, no waste, and no carbon footprint from shipping.

Top-Selling eBook Niches

Certain niches consistently perform well on Amazon:

- **Self-Help:** Motivational guides and personal development books.
- **Romance:** A massive market with subgenres like paranormal romance and historical romance.

- **Children's Books:** Interactive and educational eBooks for young readers.
- **Fantasy and Sci-Fi:** Loyal fanbases for series and standalone works.

Actionable Insight

- Use tools like **Publisher Rocket** to identify trending eBook niches.
- Test the waters by publishing short eBooks (10,000–20,000 words) to gauge reader interest.

3.2 The POD Market: Print On Your Terms

Print-on-demand technology has revolutionized the way physical books are produced and sold. With POD, you can publish a book without the risks and costs of traditional printing.

How POD Works

- Instead of printing books in bulk, POD allows books to be printed individually as orders come in.
- Amazon KDP handles the printing, packaging, and shipping, leaving you free to focus on creating content.

The Advantages of POD

- **No Inventory Costs:** You don't need to store hundreds of copies in your garage.
- **Low Risk:** Print only what you sell, reducing financial exposure.
- **Customizability:** Update your book's content or design anytime without worrying about unsold stock.

POD Market Trends

- The global POD market is projected to reach **$10 billion by 2026**.
- High-demand categories include low-content books (e.g., journals, planners) and personalized books (e.g., custom recipe books).

Popular POD Niches

- **Low-Content Books:** Planners, journals, sketchbooks, and logbooks.
- **Educational Materials:** Workbooks, study guides, and test prep books.
- **Coloring Books:** Popular with both children and adults, especially in stress-relief themes.

Actionable Insight

- Start small with low-content books to understand the POD process.
- Use **Canva** and **MidJourney** to create visually appealing designs for your books.

3.3 The Democratization of Publishing

The eBook and POD revolutions have removed traditional barriers to publishing. You no longer need a literary agent, a massive budget, or access to printing facilities. Here's how KDP levels the playing field:

Global Distribution

- Your book is available on Amazon marketplaces worldwide, reaching millions of potential readers.

- POD enables you to cater to international audiences by offering physical books in multiple regions.

Scalability and Automation

- Once your book is live, Amazon handles the logistics.
- With proper marketing, your book can generate income on autopilot.

Success Stories

- **The Planner Publisher:** A stay-at-home mom published a series of productivity planners, earning $8,000/month in royalties.
- **The Coloring Book Creator:** A small team used Canva to design adult coloring books, selling over 50,000 copies in their first year.
- **The eBook Entrepreneur:** A part-time teacher published study guides for high school students, creating a steady side income.

3.4 Why Now Is the Perfect Time to Start

The growth of the eBook and POD markets isn't slowing down—it's accelerating. Here's why you should act now:

Low Competition in Emerging Niches

While some niches like romance and self-help are saturated, others (e.g., niche planners or hyper-specific guides) remain untapped.

Technology at Your Fingertips

With AI tools like ChatGPT, Canva, and Publisher Rocket, you can compete with larger publishers on a fraction of the budget.

Reader Behavior Trends

- Increased screen time has driven demand for eBooks.
- Custom and personalized books are becoming a favorite among gift shoppers.

Actionable Insight:

The earlier you enter the market, the more likely you are to establish a foothold in profitable niches. Start with one book, learn the process, and expand from there.

Your Window of Opportunity

The eBook and POD markets are booming, and Amazon KDP is your gateway to tapping into these trends. Whether you want to create digital products, physical books, or a mix of both, the opportunities are endless.

In the next section, we'll dive into inspiring success stories to show you what's possible when you combine creativity, hard work, and the right tools.

Quick Action Exercise:

Research a niche on Amazon and note the top-performing books. What do their covers, titles, and descriptions have in common?

Brainstorm three potential niches for a POD book.

- Example: "Daily gratitude journal," "Custom fitness planner," or "Budget tracker for families."

Section 4: Inspirational Success Stories

Success Leaves Clues

Success in the world of Amazon KDP isn't reserved for seasoned authors or publishing experts. Ordinary people—students, stay-at-home parents, and entrepreneurs—are turning their ideas into books and creating life-changing income streams. In this section, we'll explore inspiring success stories, including my own journey, to show you what's possible with KDP.

4.1 My Personal Journey: From Beginner to Publisher

When I first discovered Amazon KDP, I had no experience in writing or publishing. I was hesitant, wondering if this platform could really deliver on its promise of passive income. Despite my doubts, I decided to take the plunge.

The First Book

My first book was a simple guide on time management, aimed at college students. I chose this niche because it resonated with my own experiences. Using ChatGPT, I outlined the chapters, wrote the content, and formatted the manuscript. Canva made designing the cover surprisingly easy, and Publisher Rocket helped me select keywords that made the book more discoverable.

The Breakthrough Moment

Within the first week of publishing, I earned my first $100. By the end of the month, my royalties surpassed $1,000. This wasn't just a monetary achievement—it was proof that KDP worked.

Scaling Up

Encouraged by this success, I expanded into related niches, publishing books on productivity, study techniques, and goal setting. Today, I've built a library of books that generate consistent passive income, allowing me to reinvest in my business and explore new opportunities.

4.2 The Coloring Book Moguls

The Challenge

A husband-and-wife team wanted to create a side income but had no prior publishing experience. They discovered the potential of low-content books and decided to try their hand at adult coloring books.

The Process

Using MidJourney, they generated intricate, high-quality illustrations tailored to themes like "stress relief" and "nature scenes." Canva helped them design cohesive covers that stood out in the crowded marketplace.

The Results

Their first book, *Calm in Chaos: Stress-Relief Coloring for Adults*, sold over 10,000 copies in its first year. Today, they've built a brand around their coloring books, earning over $10,000/month in royalties.

Key Takeaway

By focusing on quality designs and niche-specific themes, they turned a simple idea into a thriving business.

4.3 The Planner Prodigy

The Idea

A college student wanted to create a product that helped her peers stay organized. She decided to design a series of academic planners tailored to the unique needs of students.

The Execution

Using Canva, she designed planners that included sections for goal tracking, assignment deadlines, and exam preparation. She marketed her books on TikTok, showcasing how her planners made life easier for students.

The Outcome

Her first planner sold 1,000 copies in three months, generating $5,000 in royalties. As her social media following grew, so did her sales. She now publishes planners for professionals, teachers, and parents, diversifying her offerings.

Key Takeaway

Social media can amplify your reach, especially when your product solves a clear problem for a specific audience.

4.4 The Fiction Writer's Breakthrough

The Dream

An aspiring writer wanted to publish a sci-fi novel but felt overwhelmed by the process. Traditional publishing seemed out of reach, so she turned to Amazon KDP.

The Tools

She used ChatGPT to refine her plot and dialogue, Canva to design an eye-catching cover, and Publisher Rocket to optimize her book listing for Amazon search.

The Success

Her debut novel, *Galactic Horizons*, became a bestseller in the sci-fi category, earning her $50,000 in its first year. Encouraged by this success, she turned the book into a series, building a loyal fanbase.

Key Takeaway

Fiction writers can find immense success on KDP by leveraging AI tools and creating series that keep readers engaged.

4.5 Lessons from Real-World Success Stories

What do these success stories have in common?

1. **Focus on Niches**: Each author chose a niche they were passionate about or had identified as profitable.

2. **Leverage of AI Tools**: From ChatGPT for content creation to Canva for design, they used AI to streamline their processes.

3. **Quality Over Quantity**: Instead of rushing to publish as many books as possible, they focused on creating high-quality products that resonated with their target audience.

4. **Consistency and Marketing**: They treated their publishing efforts like a business, reinvesting in ads and social media to reach new readers.

Inspiration Meets Action

These stories show that success on Amazon KDP is achievable, regardless of your background or experience. What they all share is the willingness to take action, learn from mistakes, and scale strategically. Your story could be next.

In the next section, we'll outline the steps you need to take to start building your publishing empire. With the right mindset, tools, and strategies, you'll be well on your way to turning your ideas into a sustainable income stream.

Reflection Exercise:

1. Which of these stories inspires you the most? Why?
2. Write down one actionable takeaway you can apply to your own KDP journey.
   - Example: "I'll explore creating a planner for working professionals using Canva."

Section 5: Get Ready to Build Your Publishing Empire

The Journey Begins Here

You've seen the potential of Amazon KDP, learned how AI can streamline the process, explored the booming eBook and POD markets, and been inspired by real-world success stories. Now, it's time to take action. Building a publishing empire starts with a single step—and this book will guide you every step of the way.

5.1 Mindset: Think Like an Entrepreneur

Success in self-publishing isn't just about tools and strategies—it's about adopting the right mindset. To turn your ideas into a sustainable business, you need to think like an entrepreneur. Here's how:

1. **Embrace Learning**

Every successful publisher started as a beginner. Mistakes are inevitable, but they're also opportunities to learn and improve.

> Tip: Set aside time each week to learn a new skill, whether it's designing better covers or mastering Amazon Ads.

2. **Focus on Progress, Not Perfection**

Your first book won't be perfect, and that's okay. The key is to start. Each book you publish will teach you something new and bring you closer to your goals.

3. **Stay Consistent**

Publishing success takes time. Commit to a consistent schedule for research, writing, and publishing, and treat your KDP business like a marathon, not a sprint.

5.2 The Power of Starting Small

You don't need to publish a 500-page novel to succeed on KDP. Many successful publishers start with simple, manageable projects. Here's why starting small is powerful:

1. **Build Momentum**

A small, low-content book (like a journal or planner) is quicker to create and can give you a taste of success while building your confidence.

2. **Test the Waters**

Experimenting with smaller projects allows you to understand your audience and niche before committing to larger books.

3. **Reinvest Earnings**

The income from your first few books can be reinvested into tools, ads, or even outsourcing parts of the publishing process.

5.3 Action Plan: Your First Steps

Let's break down the first steps you need to take to start your KDP journey:

1. **Choose Your Niche**

    ☐ Think about your passions, skills, or interests.

    ☐ Use tools like ChatGPT and Publisher Rocket to research niche demand and competition.

2. **Plan Your Book**

    ☐ Outline your book's structure and content using AI.

    ☐ Decide on the format: Will it be an eBook, POD book, or both?

3. **Create Your Book**

    ☐ Write or design your book using ChatGPT, Canva, and MidJourney.

    ☐ Focus on quality, ensuring your content meets the needs of your audience.

4. **Publish and Optimize**

    ☐ Upload your book to Amazon KDP, optimizing the title, description, and keywords for maximum visibility.

    ☐ Set a competitive price based on market research.

5. **Promote Your Book**

   Start with organic marketing (e.g., social media) and gradually explore paid ads.

   Track your results and refine your strategy based on what works.

5.4 Visualizing Your Publishing Empire

Take a moment to imagine where you could be six months or a year from now. Picture yourself with a catalog of books earning consistent royalties, each one adding to your passive income stream. This isn't a far-off dream—it's achievable if you start now.

5.5 A Final Word of Motivation

Remember, the most successful authors on Amazon KDP weren't born experts. They started where you are today, with a desire to create something meaningful and the determination to see it through. The tools, strategies, and support are all here for you. Now it's your turn to take action.

"You've got the tools, the market, and the mindset—let's begin."

Take the First Step

The next chapter will dive deeper into building a strong foundation for your KDP business. You'll learn how to identify profitable niches, analyze competitors, and create books that readers love. Your publishing journey starts now.

Quick Action Exercise:

1. Write down three potential niches or topics you're interested in exploring for your first book.

2. Research those niches on Amazon to see what's trending.

3. Set a goal: Choose one idea and commit to creating your first book within 30 days.

Chapter 2: Building Your KDP Business Foundation

Section 1: Identifying Profitable Niches with AI

The Key to Success

A profitable niche is the cornerstone of a successful KDP business. Without a clear niche, your book risks being lost in the sea of content on Amazon. But with the right tools and strategies, you can find niches that are both in demand and low in competition.

In this section, we'll explore how to use AI tools to uncover niches that align with your interests and have strong market potential.

2.1.1 What Is a Niche, and Why Does It Matter?

A niche is a specific category or market segment that your book targets. Instead of trying to appeal to everyone, a good niche allows you to focus on a particular audience with unique needs or interests.

Examples of Niches:

- Broad category: "Fitness" → Niche: "Home Workouts for Busy Moms"
- Broad category: "Productivity" → Niche: "Daily Planners for Entrepreneurs"

Why It Matters:

- **Visibility:** Targeting a niche helps your book stand out in a crowded market.

- **Higher Sales Potential:** Readers are more likely to buy a book that speaks directly to their needs.

- **Easier Marketing:** A well-defined audience makes promotion more effective.

2.1.2 Using AI to Identify Profitable Niches

AI tools can simplify the process of finding niches by analyzing data and trends. Here's how to leverage these tools:

- **ChatGPT for Idea Generation**

ChatGPT can help you brainstorm niche ideas based on your interests or trending topics.

    ☐ **Prompt Example:** "Suggest five niches for a self-help book targeting young professionals."

    ☐ **Output:**

        i. Time Management for Remote Workers

        ii. Overcoming Burnout in Tech Careers

        iii. Networking for Introverts

        iv. Mindfulness for Entrepreneurs

        v. Work-Life Balance for New Parents

- **Publisher Rocket for Market Analysis** This tool provides data on Amazon's best-performing categories, keywords, and competitors.

    ☐ **Keyword Search:** Look for keywords with high search volume and low competition.

- **Category Research:** Discover subcategories where your book can rank higher.

- Google Trends for Validation

Google Trends shows the popularity of a topic over time.

- **Example:** Search for "gratitude journal" to see if interest has grown or declined in recent months.

- AI-Driven Insights from Amazon Search Bar

Use Amazon's autocomplete feature to uncover trending topics.

- Start typing "Daily Planner for..." and note the suggestions that appear.

2.1.3 The Niche Validation Process

Finding a niche is only the first step. You need to validate its profitability. Follow this process:

- Research Competitors

Look at the top-ranking books in your chosen niche.

- **Questions to Ask:**
  - Are they selling well? Check their Amazon Best Seller Rank (BSR).
  - What are their reviews saying? Identify gaps or unmet needs.

- Assess Demand

Use Publisher Rocket to check search volume for relevant keywords.

- **Tip:** A keyword with 1,000+ monthly searches indicates strong demand.

- Evaluate Competition

Avoid niches dominated by big publishers or bestsellers with thousands of reviews.

- Look for niches with books averaging 50–100 reviews, indicating manageable competition.

- Test with a Low-Content Book

Create a simple product, like a journal or workbook, to test the waters in your chosen niche.

2.1.4 Real-Life Example: Finding a Niche with AI

The Problem:

A first-time publisher wanted to create a planner but didn't know which niche to target.

The Solution:

- **Brainstormed with ChatGPT:** "Suggest niche ideas for planners."

- ChatGPT Output: "Fitness Planners for Women," "Daily Gratitude Planners," "Meal Prep Planners for Families."

- **Validated with Publisher Rocket:** The keyword "Gratitude Planner" had moderate search volume and low competition.

- **Created and Published:** A beautifully designed gratitude planner using Canva.

The Result:

The planner earned $500 in its first month, proving the niche's viability.

2.1.5 Tips for Choosing the Right Niche

- Align with Your Interests

Writing about something you enjoy or understand will make the process more enjoyable and authentic.

- Consider Evergreen Topics

Choose niches with consistent demand, such as self-help, education, or health.

- Focus on Specific Audiences

The more specific your audience, the more targeted your book can be.

   Example: "Study Planners for College Freshmen" is better than "Study Planners."

- Adapt to Trends

While evergreen niches are reliable, don't ignore trending topics that align with your skills.

The Niche Advantage

Your niche is your starting point and your competitive edge. Think of it as planting a seed in a fertile market. A great niche aligns with your interests, solves a specific problem for readers, and has the potential to generate steady sales. Let's break this process down into detailed steps.

Step 1: Understand What a Niche Is

A niche is a **focused subset of a broader market**. Instead of competing with thousands of books in a general category, you target a specific audience with unique needs or preferences.

Example:
- General Market: *Fitness Books*
- Niche: *15-Minute Home Workouts for Moms Over 40*

Why niches matter:

- **Higher Visibility:** Less competition means your book is easier to find.

- **Targeted Marketing:** A specific audience allows for focused advertising.

- **Reader Loyalty:** Readers trust authors who understand their unique needs.

Step 2: Brainstorm Niche Ideas

- Start with Your Interests and Skills

Think about what you're passionate about or knowledgeable in. This will make the creation process enjoyable and authentic.

☐ **Questions to Ask Yourself:**

- What hobbies do I enjoy? (e.g., gardening, cooking)

- What problems have I solved in my life? (e.g., managing time, losing weight)

- What am I good at? (e.g., teaching, designing, organizing)

- **Example Output:**
  - Hobbies: "Urban Gardening for Small Spaces"
  - Solved Problems: "How I Lost 20 Pounds with Intermittent Fasting"
  - Skills: "A Beginner's Guide to Graphic Design with Canva"
- **Use AI for Idea Generation**
  - **Prompt Example for ChatGPT:**

    "Suggest 10 niche ideas for self-help books targeting millennials."
  - **ChatGPT Output:**
    i. "Stress Management for Young Professionals"
    ii. "How to Build a Side Hustle in 30 Days"
    iii. "Mindfulness for Busy Parents"
- **Explore Life Experiences**

  Your personal experiences can inspire unique niches.
  - **Example:** If you struggled with procrastination in college, you could create a book like *Study Hacks for Chronic Procrastinators.*

Step 3: Research Potential Niches

Now that you have a list of ideas, it's time to validate them using research tools.

3.1 Analyze Trends with Google Trends

What It Does:

Google Trends shows the popularity of a keyword or topic over time.

How to Use It:

1. Go to Google Trends.
2. Enter your potential niche keywords.
   - Example: "Gratitude Journal" or "Meal Prep Planner."
3. Compare trends for different ideas to see which is growing in popularity.

What to Look For:

- **Steady Growth or Consistent Interest:** A niche with stable demand is ideal.
- **Seasonal Trends:** Some niches spike during certain times of the year (e.g., fitness books in January).

3.2 Evaluate Competition with Publisher Rocket

What It Does:

Publisher Rocket provides keyword and category data from Amazon, helping you analyze search volume, competition, and potential profitability.

How to Use It:

1. Open Publisher Rocket and select "Keyword Search."

2. Enter your niche idea, e.g., "Daily Planner for Teachers."

3. Analyze the results:

   Search Volume: Look for keywords with at least 1,000 searches per month.

   Competition: Avoid niches where top-ranking books have hundreds of reviews or are dominated by major publishers.

Example Output:

- Keyword: "Fitness Planner for Women"

   Monthly Searches: 2,500

   Average Reviews of Top 10 Books: 50

   Ideal Niche: Yes

3.3 Spy on Competitors

Look at existing books in your niche to understand what works and what doesn't.

1. Search for your niche on Amazon (e.g., "Productivity Planners for Moms").

2. Study the top-ranking books:

   Cover Design: What style catches attention?

   Titles and Subtitles: How do they highlight benefits?

   Reviews: What do readers praise or criticize?

Example:
A review might say, "This planner was great, but I wish it included meal prep sections." Use this feedback to create a better product.

Step 4: Validate Your Niche

After gathering data, validate your niche to ensure it's worth pursuing.

- **Demand:** Does the niche have consistent search volume or growing interest?

- **Competition:** Is the competition manageable?

    ☐ Avoid oversaturated niches (e.g., generic romance novels).

- **Profitability:** Can you price your book competitively while earning solid royalties?

Quick Test for Validation:

Create a simple low-content book (e.g., a gratitude journal) to test the niche before investing heavily in a full book.

Step 5: Choose Your Niche and Refine It

Once you've validated your niche, refine it to make it even more specific and appealing.

How to Refine:

1. Add a unique angle.

    ☐ Example: Instead of "Daily Planner," try "Daily Planner for Stay-at-Home Dads."

2. Combine niches.
    Example: "Meal Prep Planner" + "Keto Recipes" = *The Keto Meal Prep Planner for Beginners.*

Step 6: Examples of Profitable Niches

Here are some niches to inspire you:

- **Low-Content:** Gratitude journals, fitness planners, study guides.

- **Self-Help:** Time management for remote workers, confidence building for introverts.

- **Children's Books:** STEM activity books, bedtime stories with positive affirmations.

- **Fiction:** Cozy mysteries, historical romance, sci-fi for teens.

Take Action

Finding a profitable niche is the first and most crucial step to KDP success. By combining AI tools, market research, and personal interests, you can identify niches that are both meaningful and profitable.

In the next section, we'll discuss **Competitor Analysis Made Simple**, teaching you how to learn from the successes (and mistakes) of others in your chosen niche.

Deep-Dive Exercise:
1. Write down 5 topics you're passionate about.
2. Use ChatGPT to generate 5 niche ideas for each topic.

3. Validate the top 3 ideas with Google Trends and Publisher Rocket.

4. Choose 1 niche and write a short description of your ideal reader.

Section 2: Competitor Analysis Made Simple

Learn from the Best (and Worst)

Competitor analysis is the compass that guides your KDP journey. In the crowded world of self-publishing, understanding what already exists in your chosen niche is essential. It's not just about imitation—it's about innovation. By observing other books in your niche, you can identify patterns of success, uncover gaps, and craft a product that offers something truly unique to readers.

Whether you're creating a gratitude journal or writing a sci-fi novel, competitor analysis provides the insights needed to position your book as the best choice for your audience.

The Role of Competitor Analysis in KDP

Amazon KDP is a marketplace with millions of books vying for attention. Competitor analysis allows you to navigate this vast landscape with purpose. Instead of blindly publishing a book, you'll have a clear understanding of your niche, audience preferences, and what sets your book apart.

Why Competitor Analysis Matters:

- Understanding Reader Expectations:

Every niche has unspoken rules. By studying competing books, you'll learn what readers expect, whether it's the tone of writing, the type of content, or specific features like guided prompts in a journal.

- Spotting Trends and Gaps:

Competitors often reveal what's trending in your niche. For example, fitness planners might be increasingly focusing on "at-home workout tracking," while gratitude journals might now include mindfulness prompts. Identifying gaps—such as unmet reader needs or common complaints in reviews—can inspire innovative features in your book.

- Standing Out from the Crowd:

Blending in with competitors is a recipe for obscurity. Analysis helps you pinpoint how your book can stand out, whether it's through unique cover designs, better organization, or solving problems competitors overlook.

- Minimizing Risk:

Publishing a book involves time, effort, and sometimes investment. Competitor analysis reduces guesswork, ensuring that your book aligns with market demand and has a better chance of success.

What to Observe in Competitors

Competitor analysis isn't about copying—it's about learning. Each element of a competitor's book provides clues about what works and what doesn't in your chosen niche.

- Covers and Design:

Covers are often the deciding factor for potential buyers. By analyzing competitor covers, you'll notice patterns in colors, fonts, and imagery that resonate with readers. For example, planners often have clean, minimalist designs, while children's books thrive with bold, colorful illustrations. A great cover not only attracts attention but also signals quality.

- Titles and Keywords:

Titles and subtitles are where marketing meets creativity. Strong titles are concise, keyword-rich, and promise a benefit to readers. For instance, a title like *Gratitude Journal: Daily Prompts to Cultivate Positivity* instantly communicates its purpose and audience. Keywords embedded in titles and descriptions improve search visibility, making your book easier to discover.

- Content Structure and Features:

The content inside the book—whether it's guided prompts in a journal or detailed tips in a guidebook—defines its value. Competitor analysis can reveal trends like the inclusion of QR codes for downloadable resources or chapters broken into digestible sections. Incorporating these features while adding your unique twist can elevate your book.

- Reader Feedback:

Customer reviews are a treasure trove of insights. Positive reviews highlight what readers love and expect, while critical reviews point out shortcomings you can address. For example, reviews of planners often mention whether the layout is intuitive or if there's enough space for notes. Addressing these details in your book shows that you're attentive to reader needs.

Insights from Competitor Successes and Failures

Every successful book in your niche has a story to tell. From cover design to marketing strategies, each element contributes to its performance. By studying these aspects, you can incorporate proven tactics into your own approach.

Conversely, failures are equally valuable. Books with poor reviews, unappealing designs, or unclear titles teach you what to avoid. For instance, a gratitude journal with generic prompts might receive feedback like "boring" or "repetitive," signaling the need for more engaging content.

A Case Study: Lessons from the Competition

Consider a new publisher entering the niche of gratitude journals. The top-ranking books on Amazon feature calming, pastel-colored covers and titles emphasizing mindfulness. However, reviews reveal a common complaint: readers want more space for daily reflections.

By addressing this gap, the publisher creates *Gratitude Reflections: A Journal with Extra Space for Mindful Thoughts*. The result is a book that stands out not only for its beautiful cover but also for solving a problem readers frequently encounter. Within a month of launch, it earns dozens of 5-star reviews and climbs the bestseller charts.

Taking Your Competitor Analysis to the Next Level

Competitor analysis doesn't end with identifying trends. Use the insights you gather to refine your book and strategy:

•   **Combine Features Creatively:** If competitors include motivational quotes, consider pairing them with guided exercises or reflections.

•   **Refine Your Target Audience:** If reviews reveal that parents often buy planners for homeschooling, tailor your content and marketing to address their needs specifically.

•   **Leverage Marketing Insights:** If competitors successfully use bundles (e.g., selling a journal with a matching pen), explore similar add-ons or bonuses for your book.

By studying other books in your niche, you can learn what works, avoid common pitfalls, and identify opportunities to create a superior product. Think of this as your roadmap to crafting a book that stands out.

In this section, we'll break down the process of analyzing competitors, step by step.

Step 1: Identify Your Competitors

- Search for Your Niche on Amazon

   ☐ Go to the Kindle Store or Books section on Amazon.

   ☐ Enter your niche keyword (e.g., "Gratitude Journal for Moms").

   ☐ Look at the first 2–3 pages of search results.

- Example: For "Daily Planners for Teachers," you might see:

   ☐ *Teacher's Planner 2024*

- *The Organized Educator's Toolkit*
- *Weekly Lesson Plan Notebook for Teachers*

- List the Top Competitors

Create a list of the top 5–10 books based on rankings and reviews.

- Use their titles, subtitles, and covers to understand their positioning.
- Note their Amazon Best Seller Rank (BSR) to gauge sales potential.

- Pro Tip:

A BSR of under 50,000 in the Kindle Store indicates steady sales. A BSR under 10,000 is a bestseller.

Step 2: Analyze Book Covers

Your cover is your first impression—it can make or break your sales. Study your competitors' covers to identify trends and opportunities.

- What Colors and Fonts Are Popular?

- Are bright, bold colors common? Or is the design minimalist?
- For planners, clean fonts like sans-serif might dominate.

- What Imagery Is Being Used?

- Gratitude journals might feature calming visuals like flowers or abstract designs.
- Fitness books might showcase energetic images or motivational text.

- Opportunities for Differentiation:

  ☐ If most books in your niche use similar designs, consider standing out with a unique style.

  ☐ Example: Instead of a pastel cover for a gratitude journal, try a vibrant watercolor design.

Step 3: Evaluate Titles and Subtitles

A strong title and subtitle are critical for grabbing attention and boosting discoverability. Analyze your competitors' titles to see what works.

- What Formats Are Common?

  ☐ Many books use a "main title + subtitle" format:

  · *Gratitude Journal: Daily Prompts for Mindful Living*

  · *Fitness Planner: Transform Your Life in 30 Days*

- Identify Common Keywords

  ☐ Titles often include keywords that target specific audiences (e.g., "Beginners," "Women," "Kids").

- Stand Out with Specificity

  ☐ Instead of "Daily Planner," try "Daily Planner for Homeschooling Moms."

Pro Tip:

Use Publisher Rocket to find high-ranking keywords that you can incorporate into your title.

Step 4: Dive into Customer Reviews

Reviews are a goldmine of insights. They reveal what readers love, what they dislike, and what they wish was included.

- Look for Patterns in 5-Star Reviews

What features are most praised? (e.g., "The layout is simple and intuitive.")

Use this to ensure your book includes similar strengths.

- Study Critical Reviews

Identify common complaints.

- Example: "The journal is too small" or "The prompts are repetitive."

Address these weaknesses in your book.

- Create a Feedback Summary

Positive Trends: Easy-to-read fonts, motivational quotes.

Negative Trends: Lack of diversity in prompts, flimsy paper quality.

Step 5: Assess Pricing Strategies

Your pricing needs to be competitive while ensuring profitability. Study competitors' pricing to find the sweet spot.

- Analyze Price Ranges

Low-content books (e.g., planners, journals): $5.99–$14.99.

Medium-content books (e.g., guides, cookbooks): $9.99–$19.99.

- Determine What Influences Price

☐ Page count: Longer books often justify higher prices.

☐ Quality: Premium designs or unique features (e.g., spiral binding) can command more.

- Set an Introductory Price

☐ Start slightly below your competitors to attract initial buyers.

Example: If competitors are priced at $12.99, launch your book at $10.99 and increase the price once you gain reviews.

Step 6: Look Beyond Amazon

While Amazon is your primary market, don't ignore other platforms for insights.

- Check Goodreads for Reader Feedback

☐ Look at how similar books are rated and reviewed.

- Explore Social Media Trends

☐ Platforms like TikTok or Instagram can highlight trending book types in your niche.

- Analyze Book Promotion Sites

☐ Websites like BookBub or Bargain Booksy list popular books in various categories.

Step 7: Identify Opportunities to Differentiate

After gathering all this data, ask yourself:

- What can I do differently?
- How can I add more value to readers?

Examples:

- If planners often lack motivational quotes, include them in your version.

- If gratitude journals don't have enough space for reflection, add extra pages.

Real-Life Example: Competitor Analysis in Action

The Situation:

A new publisher wanted to create a gratitude journal for teens.

The Process:

1. Researched "Gratitude Journals" on Amazon and found most were generic.

2. Analyzed top competitors and noticed complaints about boring prompts.

3. Used reviews to identify a gap: Teens wanted fun, engaging designs and prompts.

4. Created a journal with bold, colorful pages and prompts tailored to teens' interests.

The Result: The book gained traction quickly, earning $1,200 in royalties within the first month.

Turn Insights into Action

Competitor analysis isn't just about studying others—it's about using their successes and failures to improve your product. By analyzing covers, titles, reviews, and pricing, you'll have the insights needed to create a standout book that resonates with your audience.

In the next section, we'll explore **Crafting Magnetic Titles and Keywords**, diving deeper into how to make your book discoverable and compelling.

Interactive Section

Action Plan:

1. Search for your niche on Amazon and list the top 5 competitors.

2. Analyze their covers, titles, and reviews.

3. Write down one improvement you can make to your book for each competitor's weakness.

Section 3: Crafting Magnetic Titles and Keywords

The Power of Words

Your title is the first impression readers have of your book. Combined with the right keywords, it determines whether your book gets noticed in Amazon's crowded marketplace or gets buried under thousands of competitors. Crafting a magnetic title and strategically embedding keywords is not just an art—it's a critical business strategy.

Titles should grab attention, convey value, and resonate with your target audience. Keywords, on the other hand, act as a compass, guiding potential readers to your book when they search on Amazon.

The Importance of a Strong Title

A strong title is more than just a name; it's a promise. It tells readers what they can expect from your book and why it's worth their time and money.

- Clarity and Specificity:

A good title clearly communicates the book's purpose or benefits. Ambiguous titles may look clever but often fail to attract clicks. For instance:

   Ambiguous: *Reflections*

   Clear: *Gratitude Journal: Daily Prompts to Cultivate Positivity*

- Emotional Connection:

A title that evokes curiosity, excitement, or a sense of urgency can make your book stand out.

   Example: *Conquer Procrastination: The 7-Day Productivity Boost*

- Audience Targeting:

A title should speak directly to its intended audience. Including specific demographics or interests can help your book appeal to the right readers.

   Example: *Meal Prep for Busy Moms: Quick and Healthy Recipes*

The Role of Subtitles

While the title captures attention, the subtitle provides additional context and highlights the unique selling points of your book. It's also an excellent opportunity to include relevant keywords.

Examples of Strong Subtitles:

•   *Fitness Planner: Transform Your Life in 30 Days with Guided Workouts and Meal Tracking*

•   *Mindfulness Journal for Teens: Prompts to Help You De-Stress, Reflect, and Find Inner Calm*

How Keywords Boost Discoverability

Keywords are the backbone of Amazon's search algorithm. When users type queries into the search bar, Amazon matches those terms with books that contain similar keywords in their titles, subtitles, and metadata. The better your keywords, the higher your book ranks in search results.

What Makes a Good Keyword?

- High Search Volume: Keywords that many users search for.
- Low Competition: Fewer books targeting the same keyword.
- Relevance: Keywords that directly relate to your book's content.

Where to Use Keywords:

- Title and Subtitle
- Book Description
- Amazon Metadata (during the publishing process)

Tools for Researching Keywords
Publisher Rocket:

This tool helps you find high-performing keywords by analyzing Amazon's data. It shows search volume, competition, and estimated earnings for books targeting specific keywords.

Amazon Search Bar Autocomplete:

Type a relevant word into Amazon's search bar, and note the suggestions that appear. These are terms real customers are searching for.

Google Trends:

Use Google Trends to analyze the popularity of specific keywords over time.

Examples of Strategic Titles and Keywords

Example 1: Gratitude Journal

- Title: *Gratitude Journal: A Daily Companion for Cultivating Positivity*

- Keywords: "gratitude journal," "positivity prompts," "daily reflections"

Example 2: Fitness Planner

- Title: *Home Fitness Planner: 30 Days to a Stronger, Healthier You*

- Keywords: "home workouts," "fitness tracker," "beginner fitness planner"

Example 3: Children's STEM Activity Book

- Title: *STEM Adventures for Kids: Fun Experiments to Spark Curiosity*

- Keywords: "STEM activities," "science experiments for kids," "fun learning"

Common Mistakes to Avoid

- Keyword Stuffing:

Overloading your title or subtitle with keywords can make it look unprofessional and unappealing.

☐ Example: *Gratitude Journal Gratitude Reflection Gratitude Prompts Daily Gratitude*

- Vague or Generic Titles:

Titles like *The Journal* or *The Planner* fail to convey the book's purpose and unique features.

- Ignoring Trends:

Trends can provide a short-term boost. For example, during a global health focus, "immune-boosting recipes" gained popularity.

Testing and Refining Your Title and Keywords

Publishing on KDP allows flexibility. If your book isn't performing well, you can tweak the title, subtitle, or keywords. Use data from sales reports and tools like Amazon Ads to test which variations perform best.

Using Publisher Rocket to Find Potential Keywords for Your Amazon KDP Book

Publisher Rocket is a powerful tool specifically designed for authors and publishers to simplify the process of keyword research, category selection, and competitor analysis on Amazon. It provides valuable data to help you identify high-performing keywords, target the right audience, and optimize your book for Amazon's search engine.

Below, I'll explain how Publisher Rocket works and how to use it effectively for keyword research.

Why Keywords Matter

Keywords are critical for making your book discoverable on Amazon. When readers search for books, Amazon's algorithm matches their search terms with the metadata of listed books. The better your keywords, the more likely your book is to appear in search results, increasing visibility and sales.

How Publisher Rocket Helps with Keywords

Publisher Rocket simplifies the keyword research process by offering:

Search Volume: See how many people search for a specific keyword each month.

Competition Score: Understand how difficult it is to rank for a keyword based on competitors.

Earnings Estimates: Discover the revenue potential of books targeting specific keywords.

Keyword Suggestions: Get additional ideas for related keywords that readers might use.

Step-by-Step Guide to Using Publisher Rocket
1. Launch the Keyword Search Feature

After logging into Publisher Rocket, navigate to the **Keyword Search** tab. This tool is designed to help you explore keywords related to your book's topic.

2. Enter Your Seed Keyword

Type a broad term related to your book's niche. For example:

• For a gratitude journal: "Gratitude," "Gratitude Journal," or "Daily Journal."

• For a fitness planner: "Workout Planner" or "Fitness Journal."

Click "Search" to generate results.

3. Analyze the Results

Publisher Rocket will display a list of keywords with the following metrics:

• **Estimated Searches/Month:** How many times this keyword is searched for on Amazon.

• **Number of Competitors:** The number of books currently ranking for this keyword.

• **Competitive Score (1–100):** A score indicating how difficult it is to rank for this keyword. Lower is better.

• **Average Monthly Earnings:** The average revenue of the top books using this keyword.

Example Output for "Gratitude Journal":

• *Gratitude Journal for Women:*

  ☐ Searches/Month: 2,500

  ☐ Competitors: 120

  ☐ Competitive Score: 45

- Avg. Monthly Earnings: $1,200
- *Gratitude Journal for Kids:*
  - Searches/Month: 800
  - Competitors: 50
  - Competitive Score: 30
  - Avg. Monthly Earnings: $900

4. Choose High-Potential Keywords

Look for keywords that strike a balance between:

- **High Search Volume:** At least 1,000 searches/month.
- **Low to Moderate Competition:** A competitive score under 50 is ideal.
- **Good Revenue Potential:** Keywords with books earning $500+ per month are worth targeting.

Tip: If a keyword has high competition but strong earnings, consider targeting a more specific variation. For instance, instead of "Gratitude Journal," try "Gratitude Journal for Busy Moms."

5. Save and Export Keywords

Once you've identified potential keywords, save them in Publisher Rocket. You can also export the list as a CSV file for easy reference when entering metadata on Amazon KDP.

Additional Features for Keyword Research

1. Amazon Search Suggestions

Publisher Rocket integrates with Amazon's autocomplete feature to suggest additional keywords that readers are actively searching for. For example, typing "Gratitude Journal" might also show:

- "Gratitude Journal for Beginners"
- "Gratitude Journal with Prompts"
- "Gratitude Journal for Teens"

2. Long-Tail Keywords

Publisher Rocket identifies long-tail keywords—phrases with three or more words. These often have lower competition but higher relevance to niche audiences.

Example:

- "Daily Gratitude Journal for Moms" vs. "Gratitude Journal."

3. Competitor Keyword Analysis

Use Publisher Rocket's **Competition Analyzer** to see which keywords top-ranking books in your niche are targeting. This helps you refine your keyword list and understand what works in your market.

How to Apply Keywords in Your Book Metadata

Title and Subtitle: Incorporate one or two primary keywords to boost discoverability without overstuffing.

☐ Example: *Gratitude Journal: Daily Prompts for Cultivating Positivity.*

Seven Keyword Slots: Amazon allows you to add up to seven backend keywords. Use variations of your top-performing keywords.

Example: "Daily Journal," "Gratitude Journal for Women," "Gratitude Prompts."

Book Description: Naturally include keywords while describing the benefits of your book.

Real-Life Example: Using Publisher Rocket for a Gratitude Journal

Scenario: You're publishing a gratitude journal for women. Using Publisher Rocket, you discover the following keywords:

• *Gratitude Journal for Women* (2,500 searches/month, low competition).

• *Mindfulness Journal for Positivity* (1,800 searches/month, moderate competition).

Result: Your title becomes: *Gratitude Journal: A Mindfulness Companion for Women to Cultivate Positivity.* Your backend keywords include:

- "Mindfulness Journal"
- "Positivity Journal"
- "Daily Reflection Journal for Women."

Within weeks of launch, your book ranks on the first page for "Gratitude Journal for Women," driving organic sales.

Publisher Rocket simplifies and accelerates the keyword research process, saving you hours of trial and error. By using its data-driven insights, you can strategically position your book to maximize visibility and sales. Whether you're a first-time publisher or scaling your KDP business, Publisher Rocket is an indispensable tool for success.

Words That Work

Crafting a magnetic title and embedding strategic keywords is one of the most impactful steps in your KDP journey. Together, they ensure your book captures attention and ranks high in Amazon search results. A well-crafted title with the right keywords doesn't just sell a book—it creates an irresistible promise for readers.

In the next section, we'll focus on **Setting Up an Amazon KDP Account**, guiding you through the technical and practical steps to get started.

Using BookBeam for Keyword and Niche Research in KDP

BookBeam is another powerful tool that focuses on data-driven insights for authors and publishers. It's particularly helpful for finding keywords, analyzing book niches, and optimizing your product listing. Its advanced analytics make it a strong companion for authors who want to maximize their visibility and revenue on Amazon.

Below, I'll explain how BookBeam works and how you can use it effectively for both keyword and niche research.

Why BookBeam?

BookBeam stands out because it provides deep insights into:

Keyword Performance: Search volume, competition, and revenue potential for specific keywords.

Niche Analysis: Identifies trending niches and assesses their profitability.

Category Insights: Shows which categories are underutilized and ripe for ranking.

Historical Data: Tracks keyword and niche performance over time, helping you stay ahead of trends.

How BookBeam Helps with Keyword Research

Keywords are vital for ensuring your book is discoverable on Amazon. BookBeam simplifies keyword research by:

•	Identifying high-performing keywords with detailed data.

•	Showing long-tail keywords that target specific audiences.

•	Highlighting low-competition keywords for easier ranking.

Step-by-Step Guide to Using BookBeam

1. Exploring Keyword Research

BookBeam's Keyword Research feature provides actionable insights into which terms readers are searching for.

Access the Keyword Tool:

☐ Navigate to the Keyword Research section on BookBeam's dashboard.

Enter a Seed Keyword:

Start with a broad keyword related to your niche (e.g., "Fitness Planner" or "Gratitude Journal").

Analyze Keyword Results:

BookBeam displays key metrics for each keyword, including:

☐ **Search Volume:** The average number of searches per month.

☐ **Competition:** A rating that shows how hard it is to rank for that keyword.

☐ **Revenue Potential:** The average monthly income for books targeting this keyword.

☐ **Keyword Trends:** Historical data showing how the keyword has performed over time.

Example Output for "Gratitude Journal":

- *Gratitude Journal for Moms*
  - ☐ Search Volume: 3,000
  - ☐ Competition: Low
  - ☐ Revenue Potential: $2,500/month
- *Gratitude Journal with Prompts*
  - ☐ Search Volume: 1,500
  - ☐ Competition: Medium
  - ☐ Revenue Potential: $1,200/month

2. Discover Long-Tail Keywords

BookBeam excels at finding long-tail keywords—specific phrases with lower competition but strong relevance.

Example:

•   Instead of "Fitness Planner," you might discover "30-Day Fitness Planner for Beginners."

•   Instead of "Gratitude Journal," consider "Gratitude Journal for Busy Professionals."

3. Prioritize Keywords

Once you have a list of keywords, prioritize them based on:

•   **Search Volume:** Focus on terms with high search activity.

•   **Low Competition:** Target less competitive keywords for easier ranking.

•   **Relevance:** Choose keywords that match your book's content.

Using BookBeam for Niche Research

Finding the right niche can be the difference between a successful book and one that struggles to sell. BookBeam provides tools to help you assess niches for profitability and competition.

1. Identify Trending Niches

BookBeam tracks emerging trends and shows which niches are gaining popularity.

How to Use It:

Go to the Niche Explorer section.

Enter a broad category, such as "Self-Help" or "Children's Books."

Review niche suggestions based on search volume, revenue potential, and competition.

Example:
- Trending Niche: "Mindfulness for Teens."
  - Search Volume: 2,000/month.
  - Average Revenue: $4,000/month.
  - Competition: Low.

2. Validate Niche Profitability

Use BookBeam's data to validate whether a niche is worth pursuing. Focus on niches with:

- **Steady Demand:** Search volume that remains consistent or grows over time.
- **Low Competition:** Fewer books dominating the space.
- **Reader Engagement:** Positive reviews and strong ratings in competing books.

Analyzing Categories with BookBeam

Amazon allows you to select two categories for your book, and choosing the right ones can boost your book's visibility. BookBeam provides data on which categories are easiest to rank in.

Explore Category Performance:

- Search for categories related to your niche.

- BookBeam shows the average BSR (Best Seller Rank) for books in that category, helping you gauge competitiveness.

Choose Underserved Categories:

- Look for categories where books have high rankings despite lower competition.

- Example: Instead of targeting "Self-Help," consider a subcategory like "Journaling for Mental Health."

Monitor Category Trends:

- BookBeam tracks how categories perform over time, ensuring you align with growing markets.

Real-Life Example: Using BookBeam for a Gratitude Journal

Scenario:
You're planning to publish a gratitude journal but want to ensure it targets a profitable niche.

Steps Taken with BookBeam:

1. Entered "Gratitude Journal" into the Keyword Tool.
2. Discovered long-tail keywords like:
   - *Gratitude Journal for Moms*
   - *Mindfulness Journal for Busy Professionals.*
3. Analyzed niche profitability using the Niche Explorer tool:

☐ Chose "Mindfulness for Teens" due to its low competition and high revenue potential.

4. Selected categories using the Category Explorer:

☐ Added "Self-Help for Teens" and "Mental Health Journals" for better discoverability.

Result:
Your book, *Mindfulness Journal for Teens: Prompts to Reduce Stress and Cultivate Positivity,* ranks on the first page of its categories within a month, earning $1,800 in the first 30 days.

BookBeam's Key Features at a Glance

- **Keyword Insights:** Provides search volume, competition, and trends for precise keyword targeting.

- **Niche Explorer:** Identifies trending and profitable niches for new book ideas.

- **Category Explorer:** Helps you find the best categories for ranking and discoverability.

- **Competitor Analysis:** Analyzes top-performing books to highlight what works in your chosen niche.

Tips for Maximizing BookBeam's Potential

- **Combine with Other Tools:** Use BookBeam alongside Publisher Rocket to cross-validate data.

- **Monitor Trends Regularly:** Set a schedule to revisit BookBeam insights to stay updated on keyword and niche shifts.

- **Focus on Long-Tail Keywords:** These often lead to higher conversions as they target specific reader needs.

Harnessing BookBeam for KDP Success

BookBeam is a powerful ally in your KDP journey, helping you identify the best keywords, niches, and categories with precision. By leveraging its data, you can optimize your book's discoverability, align with reader demand, and increase your chances of ranking and earning consistently.

Exploring the Coloring Book Niche on Amazon KDP

Coloring books have become a thriving niche on Amazon KDP, offering creators a unique opportunity to tap into an ever-growing market. From kids' activity books to stress-relief coloring books for adults, the demand for well-designed coloring books spans diverse audiences. Here's an in-depth guide to understanding and succeeding in this niche.

Why the Coloring Book Niche Is Lucrative
Diverse Audience:

- Kids: Parents often buy coloring books as educational and entertaining tools.

- Adults: Stress-relief and mindfulness-themed coloring books are popular among professionals and hobbyists.

High Demand for Low-Content Products:

Coloring books are considered low-content products, meaning they don't require extensive writing. This makes them easier and quicker to create.

Creative Potential:

- Artists and designers can showcase unique styles.
- Creators with no artistic skills can use AI tools to generate stunning designs.

Repeat Purchases:

Unlike novels or guides, coloring books are consumable. Readers often buy multiple books within a niche or by the same creator.

Top Niches within the Coloring Book Category

Children's Coloring Books:

- Alphabet and Numbers: For preschool and kindergarten kids.
- Animals: Dinosaurs, zoo animals, pets.
- Themes: Princesses, trucks, space, and superheroes.

Adult Coloring Books:

- Stress-Relief: Mandalas, floral patterns, abstract designs.
- Mindfulness: Inspirational quotes with intricate patterns.
- Themed Collections: Fantasy, horror, mythology, and seasonal designs.

Specialty Coloring Books:

- Educational: Geography maps, anatomy illustrations.
- Activity-Based: Puzzles combined with coloring.
- Personalized: Customizable names or messages.

Seasonal Coloring Books:

- Holidays: Christmas, Halloween, Easter.
- Seasons: Winter, Spring, Summer, Fall.

How to Research the Coloring Book Niche

1. Keyword Research

Keywords are critical for identifying profitable coloring book ideas and optimizing listings.

Use Publisher Rocket or BookBeam:

Search for keywords like "stress relief coloring book" or "kids dinosaur coloring book." Analyze metrics like search volume and competition.

Explore Amazon Search Bar Suggestions:

Type "coloring book for…" into Amazon's search bar to discover popular terms. Examples:

- "Coloring book for toddlers age 2-4."
- "Coloring book for adults relaxation."

Analyze Competitors' Keywords:

Look at bestselling books in your niche and identify keywords they're targeting.

2. Competitor Analysis

Study the top-ranking coloring books in your niche to learn what works.

Covers and Titles:

- Bright, bold designs with clear themes.
- Titles like *Big Dinosaur Coloring Book for Kids* or *Calm & Relax: Adult Mandala Coloring Book*.

Pricing:

Most children's coloring books are priced between $5.99–$8.99. Adult coloring books often range from $7.99–$12.99, depending on complexity.

Content and Reviews:

- Check reviews for feedback on design quality, page thickness, and usability.
- Look for gaps, such as "not enough designs" or "too small images."

How to Create a Coloring Book

Creating a coloring book doesn't require professional design skills. Here's how to do it:

1. Generate Illustrations

Hire a Designer:

Platforms like Fiverr or Upwork can connect you with professional artists.

Use AI Tools:

Tools like **MidJourney** and **Leonardo.ai** can create intricate, high-quality designs. For example:

- Mandalas for adults.
- Cartoon-style animals for kids.

Use Pre-Made Assets:

Websites like Creative Fabrica or Etsy offer design bundles for commercial use.

2. Formatting the Book

Page Size:

- Standard size: 8.5 x 11 inches (perfect for kids and adults).
- Ensure designs have sufficient margins for printing.

Page Content:

- Black-and-white illustrations suitable for coloring.
- Consider adding blank pages on the back of designs to prevent bleed-through.

Software Tools:

- Canva: Ideal for beginners.
- Adobe Illustrator or Inkscape: For advanced customization.
- Affinity Publisher: Great for combining illustrations and formatting.

3. Adding Value

Themes and Series:

Create a consistent style and theme to build a loyal audience.

- Example: A series of "Relax & Color" books featuring floral, abstract, and scenic themes.

Bonus Features:

- Inspirational quotes.
- QR codes for downloadable content.

Marketing Your Coloring Book

Optimize Your Listing:

- Use keywords in the title, subtitle, and description.
- Highlight the benefits: "Perfect for stress relief and relaxation."

Promote on Social Media:

- Instagram and Pinterest are great platforms for showcasing designs.
- Share time-lapse videos of someone coloring pages from your book.

Leverage Amazon Ads:

- Start with low bids targeting specific keywords (e.g., "adult stress relief coloring book").

Bundle Your Books:

- Offer two or more books together for a discounted price.

Real-Life Example: Coloring Book Success Story

Scenario:

A new publisher wanted to create a coloring book targeting adults interested in mindfulness.

Steps Taken:

- Keyword Research:

Found "mandala coloring book stress relief" had high search volume and low competition.

- Design Creation:

Used MidJourney to generate 50 unique mandalas.

- Unique Angle:

Added inspirational quotes on every page, appealing to mindfulness enthusiasts.

- Launch Strategy:

Priced the book at $8.99 with a 7-day Amazon Ads campaign targeting "mindfulness coloring books."

Result: The book sold 300 copies in its first month, earning $2,000 in royalties and establishing the publisher in the niche.

Challenges in the Coloring Book Niche

- Competition: The market can be crowded, so focus on a specific audience or unique style.

- Printing Quality:

Amazon's print-on-demand service can sometimes result in minor inconsistencies. Ensure your designs are optimized for their specifications.

- Copyright Issues:

Always use original or licensed assets to avoid infringement.

The Endless Opportunities of Coloring Books

The coloring book niche is vibrant and full of potential. By identifying a specific audience, creating unique designs, and leveraging tools like BookBeam or Publisher Rocket for research, you can establish a successful and sustainable business on Amazon KDP. Creativity, research, and consistent quality are the keys to dominating this lucrative niche.

Exploring the Storybook Niche on Amazon KDP

Storybooks have been a timeless favorite for readers, making them an evergreen and highly profitable niche on Amazon KDP. Whether you're targeting children, teens, or adults, storybooks allow creators to connect with audiences on an emotional level, fostering creativity and imagination.

Here's an in-depth look at how to navigate and succeed in the storybook niche.

Why the Storybook Niche Is a Great Choice

- Broad Audience Appeal:

　　◻ Children's storybooks are staples for families and educators.

　　◻ Teen and young adult fiction thrives in genres like fantasy, romance, and sci-fi.

Adults often gravitate toward short stories, inspirational tales, or niche fiction.

- Global Reach:

Stories transcend cultural and language barriers, offering opportunities for international sales or translations.

- Evergreen Demand:

Storybooks, especially for children, remain relevant across generations.

- High Engagement:

Readers often recommend or gift storybooks, creating organic growth.

Top Niches within the Storybook Category

- Children's Storybooks:

 Picture Books (Ages 3-5): Focused on illustrations with simple text. Common themes: friendship, animals, or bedtime stories.

 Early Readers (Ages 6-8): Stories with basic vocabulary and engaging characters.

 Middle-Grade Fiction (Ages 9-12): Stories with more complexity, such as adventures or moral lessons.

- Teen and Young Adult Fiction (YA):

 Fantasy and Adventure: Worlds with magic, quests, and mythical creatures.

 Romance: High school dramas, coming-of-age love stories.

- **Dystopian and Sci-Fi:** Exploring futuristic societies or survival themes.

- **Adult Storybooks:**

  - **Short Stories:** Bite-sized tales in genres like mystery, thriller, or literary fiction.

  - **Inspirational Stories:** Focusing on themes of hope, resilience, and life lessons.

  - **Humorous Stories:** Lighthearted collections perfect for casual readers.

- **Cultural and Folk Tales:**

  - Retelling of myths, legends, or traditional stories with modern twists.

  - Example: *Greek Myths Retold for Teens*.

How to Research the Storybook Niche

1. Keyword and Market Research

Finding the right keywords and understanding your audience is crucial for success.

Publisher Rocket/BookBeam for Keywords:

Search for terms like:

- "Bedtime stories for kids"
- "YA fantasy book series"
- "Inspirational short stories"

Analyze Competitor Listings:

- Study bestselling storybooks in your target niche.

Pay attention to their titles, covers, and subtitles.

Amazon Categories:

Browse through relevant categories like:

"Children's Books > Fairy Tales"

"Young Adult Books > Fantasy & Magic"

"Literature & Fiction > Short Stories."

2. Audience Trends

Children's Preferences:

Parents and educators look for moral lessons, imaginative worlds, or bedtime stories.

Example: Books like *The Gruffalo* and *Goodnight Moon*.

Teen Trends:

YA fiction is influenced by social themes, diversity, and character-driven plots.

Example: *The Hunger Games* or *To All the Boys I've Loved Before*.

Adult Readers:

Adults often seek quick reads or thought-provoking content.

Example: *Chicken Soup for the Soul* or short stories by Haruki Murakami.

How to Create a Storybook

1. Crafting the Story

Start with a Hook:

    ☐ An engaging opening draws readers in immediately.

    ☐ Example: "In the heart of an enchanted forest, a timid rabbit discovered a magical amulet…"

Build Relatable Characters:

    ☐ Create characters readers can connect with, regardless of age.

    ☐ For children: A talking dog who learns teamwork.

    ☐ For teens: A misunderstood high schooler navigating friendships.

Follow the Classic Story Arc:

    ☐ **Beginning:** Introduce the setting, characters, and conflict.

    ☐ **Middle:** Build tension and challenges.

    ☐ **End:** Resolve the conflict with a satisfying conclusion.

Incorporate a Theme or Moral:

    ☐ Example for kids: "The value of sharing."

    ☐ Example for teens: "Overcoming self-doubt."

2. Illustrations for Children's Books

Children's books rely heavily on visuals to captivate their audience.

Hire an Illustrator:

    ☐ Platforms like Fiverr, Upwork, or Behance offer talented illustrators for custom designs.

Use AI Tools:

MidJourney, DALL·E, or Leonardo.ai can create vibrant illustrations with unique styles.

Style Consistency:

Maintain a uniform style throughout the book to ensure visual coherence.

Example: Watercolor designs for bedtime stories, bold lines for action-packed tales.

3. Formatting the Storybook

Page Size:

Standard children's books: 8.5 x 8.5 inches (square format).

Middle-grade or YA fiction: 5.5 x 8.5 inches or 6 x 9 inches.

Text and Font:

Large, easy-to-read fonts for younger readers.

For teens and adults, use elegant fonts with proper line spacing.

Software Tools:

Canva: For simple layouts and illustrations.

Adobe InDesign: Professional-level formatting.

Marketing and Monetizing Storybooks

1. Optimize Your Amazon Listing

Title and Subtitle:

☐ Example: *Sleepy Adventures: A Bedtime Storybook to Inspire Sweet Dreams.*

☐ Keywords: "bedtime stories," "inspire sweet dreams."

Description:

☐ Highlight what makes the story special, such as illustrations, themes, or audience benefits.

Categories and Keywords:

☐ Choose categories that align with your book's themes.

2. Social Media and Influencer Outreach

Leverage Instagram and TikTok:

☐ Share snippets of illustrations or short videos about the story.

Collaborate with Bloggers:

☐ Children's books can gain traction through parenting blogs or teacher networks.

3. Expand to Other Platforms

Audible and Audiobooks:

☐ Record narrated versions for children or YA fiction.

☐ Example: *Bedtime stories with soothing narrations.*

Bundle Series:

☐ Offer storybook series for a discounted price.

Real-Life Example: Storybook Success Story

Scenario: A self-publisher wanted to create a storybook for young readers about bravery and teamwork.

Steps Taken:

1. Wrote a 20-page story about a young dragon learning to overcome fear.

2. Hired an illustrator to create vibrant, child-friendly artwork.

3. Marketed the book to parenting blogs and Instagram influencers.

Result: The book, *The Brave Little Dragon,* became a bestseller in the "Children's Books on Friendship" category, selling over 1,000 copies in three months.

Challenges in the Storybook Niche

- High Competition:

Many established authors and publishers dominate this niche. Focus on unique angles or underserved audiences.

- Illustration Costs:

Professional artwork can be expensive, but tools like AI can help mitigate costs.

- Lengthy Production Time:

Storybooks often take longer to create due to illustrations and detailed editing.

Storybooks as a Long-Term Investment

The storybook niche offers immense creative freedom and evergreen potential. With a compelling story, captivating illustrations, and strategic marketing, you can create books that resonate with readers of all ages. Whether you're crafting bedtime stories for toddlers or YA novels for teens, the key to success lies in understanding your audience and consistently delivering value.

Section 4: Setting Up Your Amazon KDP Account

Your Gateway to Publishing Success

Amazon KDP (Kindle Direct Publishing) is the platform that enables you to self-publish eBooks, paperbacks, and hardcovers, making your work available to readers across the globe. Setting up your KDP account is the first and most crucial step in this journey. A well-configured account ensures smooth operations, accurate royalty payments, and access to Amazon's vast marketplace.

This section provides a detailed, step-by-step guide to setting up your Amazon KDP account, avoiding common pitfalls, and optimizing your setup for success.

Why Setting Up Your KDP Account Properly Is Important

Streamlined Publishing Process:

A properly set up account minimizes errors during uploads and publication.

Accurate Payments:

Ensures that your royalties are deposited on time and in the correct currency.

Global Reach:

Enables you to sell books in multiple regions with appropriate tax and legal compliance.

Step 1: Create Your KDP Account

Visit the KDP Website:

- Navigate to https://kdp.amazon.com.
- Click on **Sign Up** if you don't have an account or **Sign In** if you already have an Amazon account.

Link Your Amazon Account:

- If you already have an Amazon shopping account, you can use it for KDP.
- Otherwise, create a new account by providing:
  - A valid email address.
  - A strong password.
  - Verification details (email and mobile phone number).

Accept Terms and Conditions:

- Review and accept Amazon's KDP terms to proceed.

Step 2: Complete Your Profile

Personal or Business Information:

- Decide if you're publishing as an individual or a business.
- Enter your legal name, address, and phone number.

Bank Account Details for Payments:

- Provide accurate banking information for royalty deposits.
- If you're outside the US:
  - Use an account that supports ACH or SWIFT transfers.
  - Double-check IBAN or SWIFT codes for accuracy.

Tax Information:

- Complete the online tax interview to ensure compliance with IRS and local tax laws.
- For US authors:
  - Provide your Social Security Number (SSN) or Employer Identification Number (EIN).
- For non-US authors:
  - Fill out a W-8BEN form to claim tax treaty benefits and avoid excessive withholding.

Pro Tip: Consult a tax professional if you're unsure about the required information.

Step 3: Explore the KDP Dashboard

The KDP dashboard is the control panel for your publishing journey. Familiarizing yourself with its features is essential.

Bookshelf:

⬜ Add new books or edit existing ones.

⬜ Monitor the status of your titles (e.g., draft, under review, published).

Reports:

⬜ Track sales, royalties, and page reads for Kindle Unlimited.

Community:

⬜ Access forums, tutorials, and FAQs for troubleshooting and tips.

Marketing Tools:

⬜ Manage Amazon Ads and promotional tools, such as Kindle Countdown Deals and Free Promotions.

Step 4: Set Up Your Publishing Preferences

1. Publishing Formats:

- Decide which formats you want to publish: eBook, paperback, or hardcover.
- Each format has specific setup requirements (e.g., interior formatting, cover design).

2. Language Options:

- Choose your book's primary language. KDP supports over 40 languages for eBooks.

3. Global Rights:

- Select where you want your book to be sold.

- Choose "Worldwide Rights" to maximize your reach unless you have exclusive territorial agreements.

4. Pricing and Royalties:

- eBooks:

    ☐ 35% royalty for books priced under $2.99 or above $9.99.

    ☐ 70% royalty for books priced between $2.99 and $9.99 in eligible markets.

- Paperbacks and Hardcovers:

    ☐ Set a list price that covers printing costs while ensuring a healthy profit margin.

Pro Tip: Use Amazon's royalty calculator to estimate earnings and printing costs.

Step 5: Upload a Test Book

Before diving into full-fledged publishing, upload a test book to familiarize yourself with the process.

Prepare a Placeholder File:

☐ Use a simple Word document with placeholder text to simulate an eBook upload.

☐ For paperbacks, prepare a basic PDF file.

Upload the File:

☐ Navigate to the "Bookshelf" tab and click **Add New Title**.

☐ Follow the prompts to upload your manuscript and cover.

Review the Preview:

  Use the KDP Previewer to check for formatting errors.

  Ensure that text, images, and margins appear as intended.

Step 6: Troubleshooting Common Issues

Payment Issues:

  Ensure your bank account is verified and supports international payments if applicable.

Tax Verification Delays:

  Check that all tax details match official documents.

  Contact KDP support if processing exceeds the stated timeline.

File Upload Errors:

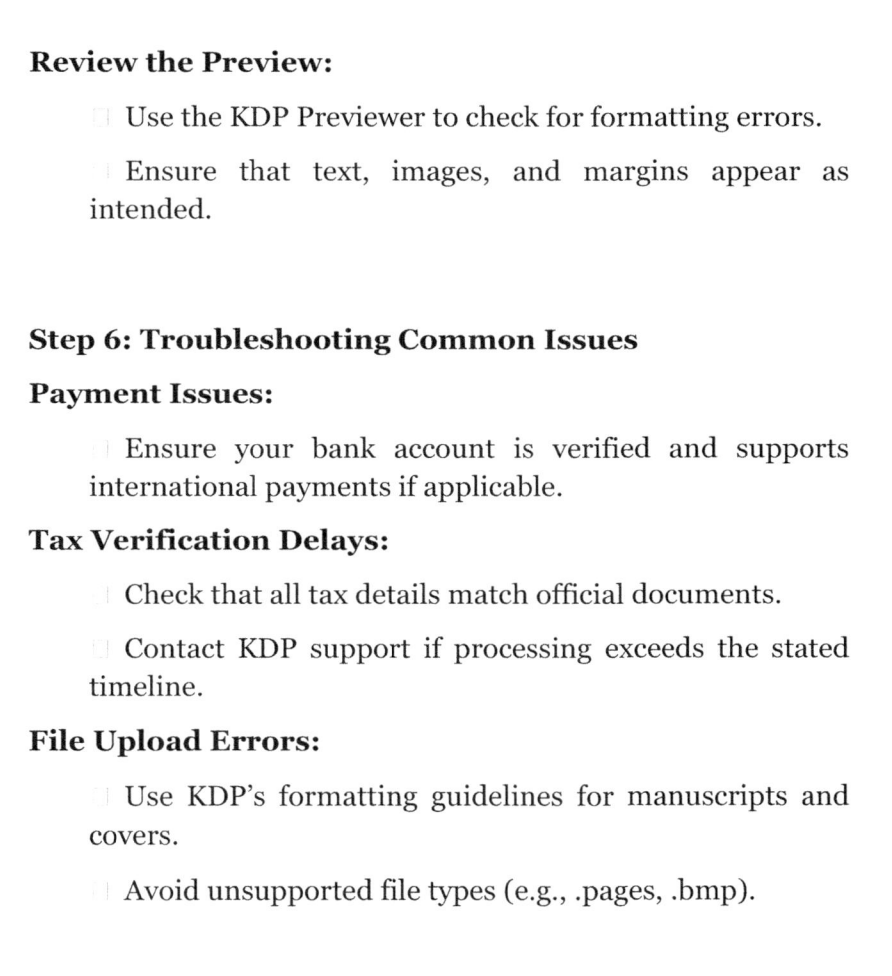

  Use KDP's formatting guidelines for manuscripts and covers.

  Avoid unsupported file types (e.g., .pages, .bmp).

Step 7: Optimize Your Account for Long-Term Success

1. Regularly Update Payment Information:

•   Keep your bank and tax details current to avoid disruptions.

2. Monitor Reports:

•   Analyze sales trends to identify high-performing books and adjust strategies.

3. Engage with the KDP Community:

- Participate in forums to learn from experienced authors and publishers.

Key Tools and Resources for Setting Up Your KDP Account

Amazon KDP Help Center:

☐ Comprehensive guides and FAQs for account setup.

YouTube Tutorials:

☐ Step-by-step videos on setting up accounts and publishing books.

Tax and Banking Consultants:

☐ Professional advice for complex tax or payment setups.

Your First Step Toward Passive Income

Setting up your Amazon KDP account is the foundation of your publishing business. By following these detailed steps and addressing common challenges, you'll ensure a seamless start to your self-publishing journey. With your account ready, you're all set to publish your first book and begin building a sustainable income stream.

Section 5: Laying the Groundwork for Long-Term Success

Building a Sustainable KDP Business

The foundation of a successful Amazon KDP business is more than publishing a single book—it's about creating a strategy that ensures consistent growth, reader retention, and sustainable income. In this section, we'll explore how to build a long-term content strategy, develop your author brand, and ensure your publishing efforts have lasting impact.

1. Develop a Content Strategy

Why Content Strategy Matters

A content strategy is your roadmap to creating books that align with reader demand while maximizing your profitability. It helps you plan what to publish, when to publish, and how to expand your catalog.

Key Elements of a Content Strategy:

Identify Your Core Niche:

- Build your expertise in a specific area (e.g., coloring books, self-help guides, or children's storybooks).
- Example: If you're publishing journals, focus on niches like fitness, mindfulness, or productivity.

Plan for Series:

- Create books that form part of a series. Readers who love one book are more likely to purchase the rest.
- Example: A series of children's storybooks featuring the same character, such as *Tales of Benny the Brave Bunny*.

Experiment with Formats:

- Explore different formats like eBooks, paperbacks, hardcovers, and audiobooks to reach diverse audiences.

Include Seasonal Books:

☐ Publish books tied to holidays or events (e.g., *Christmas Coloring Book for Kids*).

Pro Tip: Use AI tools like ChatGPT to brainstorm book ideas and plan content outlines for upcoming titles.

2. Build Your Author Brand

Why Branding Matters

A strong author brand establishes trust and recognition. Readers are more likely to buy books from authors they trust or follow.

Steps to Build Your Author Brand:

Create an Author Website:

☐ Include a blog, book listings, and links to your Amazon page.

☐ Example: *www.YourAuthorName.com*.

Engage on Social Media:

☐ Share updates, behind-the-scenes content, and interact with your audience.

☐ Platforms like Instagram, TikTok, and Pinterest are great for visually engaging content like coloring books and journals.

Develop a Consistent Voice:

☐ Whether it's inspirational, humorous, or professional, maintain a consistent tone across your books and marketing materials.

Leverage Email Marketing:

- Build an email list by offering free resources or bonuses (e.g., downloadable worksheets or coloring pages).

- Send newsletters to announce new releases or share exclusive content.

3. Focus on Reader Retention

How to Keep Readers Coming Back

- Series Strategy:

- Create cliffhangers or interconnected stories in fiction books.

- In non-fiction, add "next steps" that lead readers to another book in your catalog.

- Engage Through Bonus Content:

- Include links to free downloadable materials like printables, eBooks, or exclusive chapters.

- Encourage Reviews:

- Ask readers to leave reviews at the end of your book.

- Offer a simple call-to-action, like: *"If you enjoyed this book, consider leaving a review to help others discover it!"*

- Personal Touch:

- Add an author's note or personal story to connect with readers on a deeper level.

4. Diversify Your Income Streams

Go Beyond Amazon KDP

- **Sell Directly to Readers:**

    ☐ Use platforms like Gumroad, Etsy, or your own website to sell printable or physical copies of your books.

- **Expand to Audiobooks:**

    ☐ Create audiobooks using platforms like ACX or Findaway Voices.

- **Affiliate Marketing:**

    ☐ Recommend tools, books, or resources related to your niche through affiliate links.

- **Create Digital Products:**

    ☐ Convert your books into courses, webinars, or workshops.

    ☐ Example: A mindfulness journal author can create a mindfulness coaching program.

5. Track and Optimize Performance

Why Analytics Matter

Analyzing your book's performance helps you identify what works and refine your approach for future projects.

Metrics to Monitor:

- **Sales Trends:**

    ☐ Track which books perform well during specific times (e.g., holidays).

- **Advertising ROI:**

Measure the effectiveness of Amazon Ads and adjust campaigns based on performance.

- Reader Feedback:

Use reviews to identify strengths and areas for improvement in your books.

Tools to Use:

- Amazon KDP Reports: Sales and royalty data.
- BookBeam or Publisher Rocket: Keyword and category performance.
- Google Analytics: Monitor traffic to your author website.

Lay a Foundation for Success

Building a long-term KDP business requires strategic planning, consistent branding, and a focus on delivering value to your readers. By developing a solid content strategy, engaging with your audience, and diversifying your revenue streams, you can create a sustainable publishing empire that thrives for years to come.

INSTRUCTIONS FOR CREATING AN AMAZON KDP ACCOUNT

1. First, you need to prepare a document to verify your identity such as: Citizen ID, driver's license or passport.

2. An account to receive $ (royalties) from Amazon (create a Lian Lian global account)

3. Personal phone number.

Instructions for creating a LianLian account:

Step 1: access the website lianlianglobal.com

On the homepage, select login:

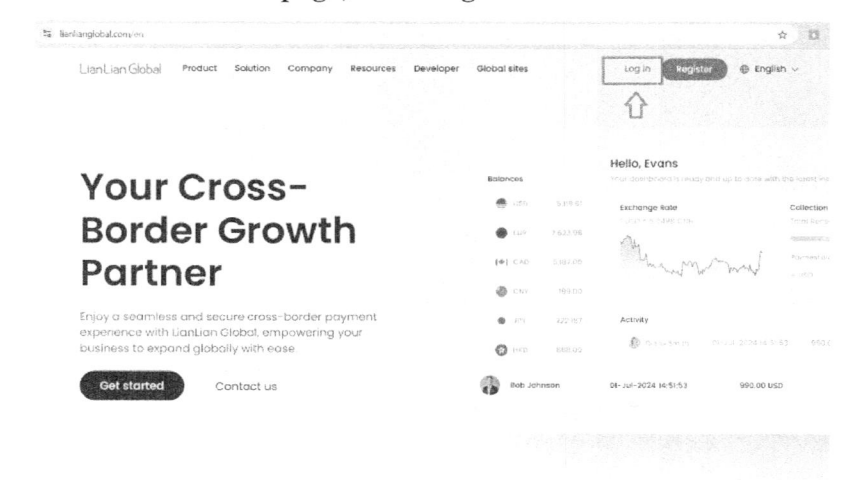

Step 2: On the login page: if you do not have an account, select register.

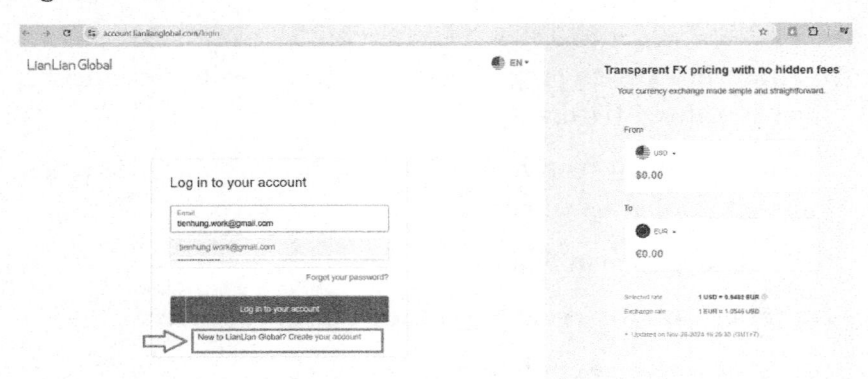

Step 3: Fill in all required information: select individual, enter registration email, enter phone number and press send code.

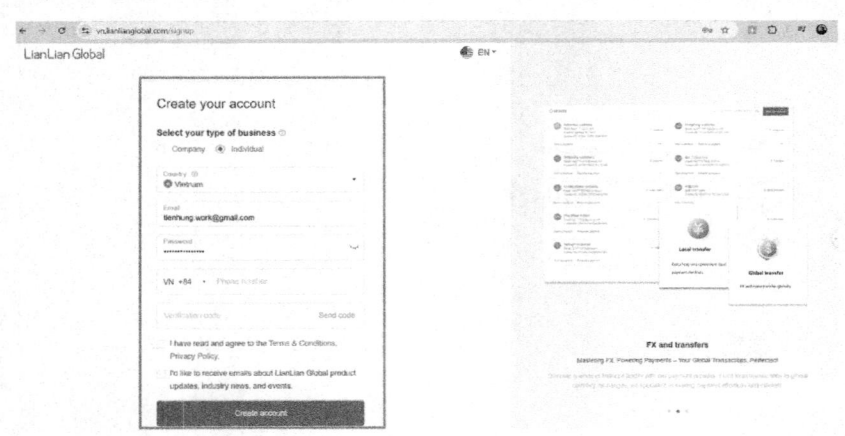

Step 4: After filling in all the information and entering the code, choose to create a new account:

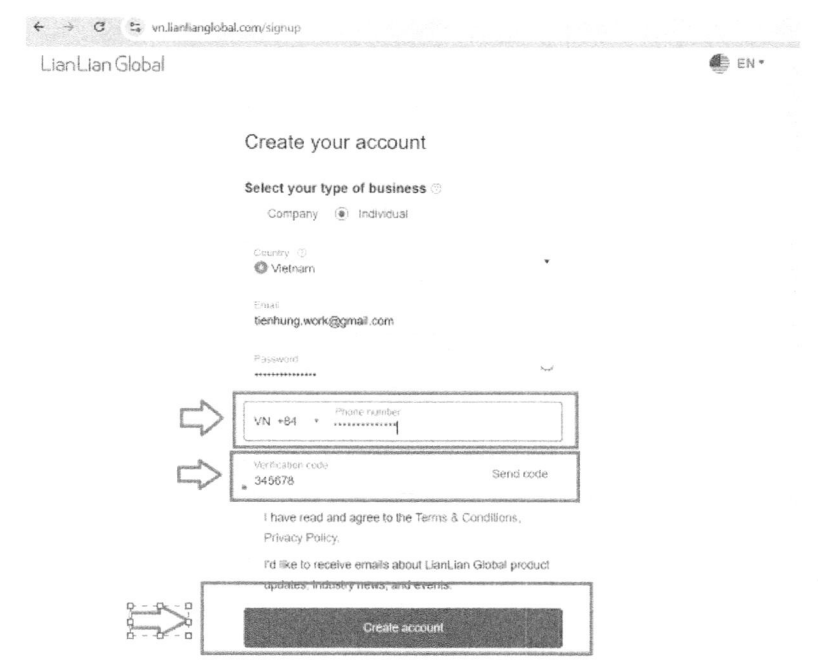

After choosing to create a new account, you will receive a registration confirmation email.

Step 5: At the personal information filling interface: fill in all the information (First name, Middle name, Last name, Date, Permanent address, postal code, we go to google to look it up.

Step 6: After filling in all the information, we choose to send. On the home page interface, we need to verify the account.

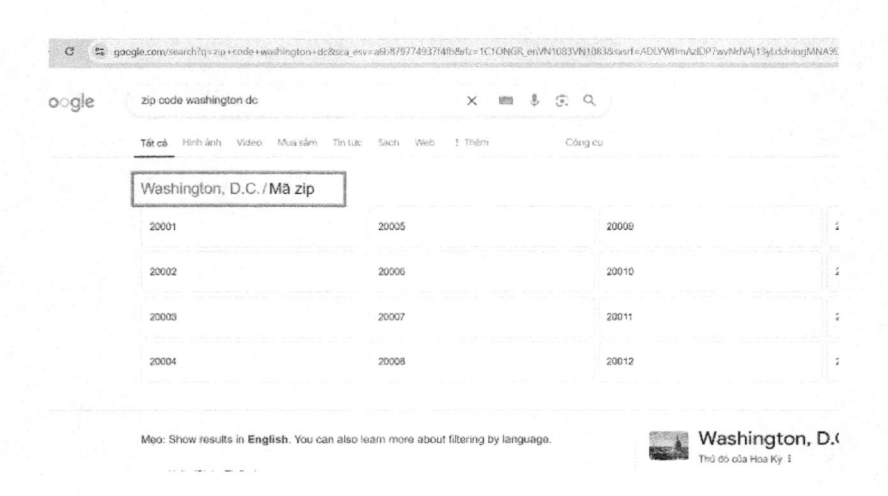

AI Publishing Profits

Account verification steps: check information again and proceed with identity verification.

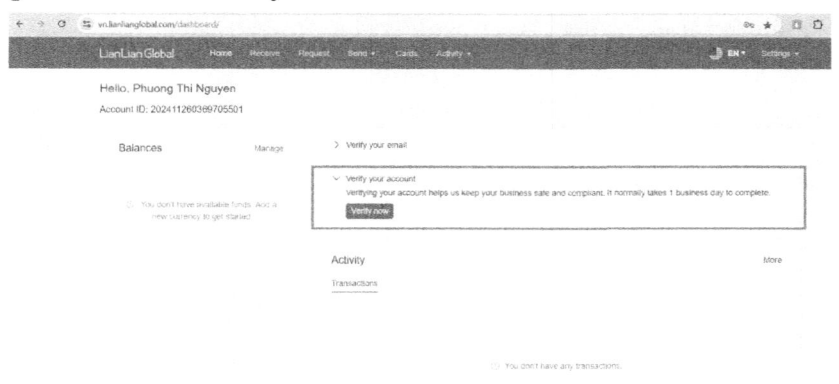

Step 7: Use your phone to scan the QR code and take a photo of both sides of your CCCD and your face.

After the scan is successful, select continue.

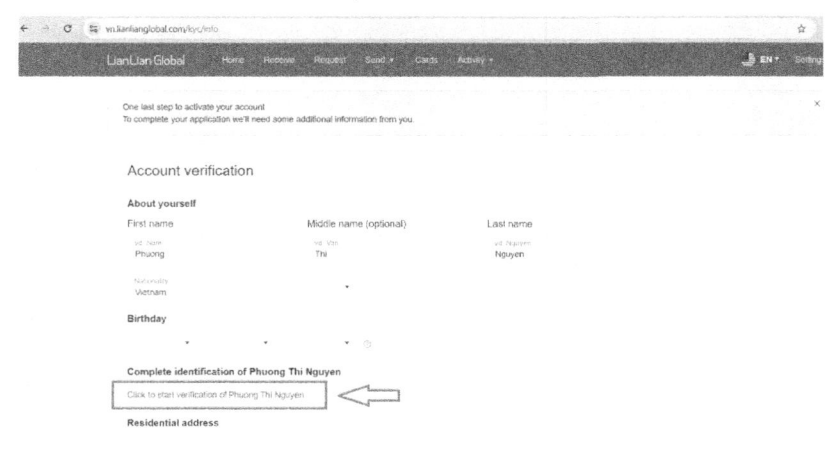

Step 8: In the address verification section, we can select bank statement and proceed to upload the statement file. After filling in all the information, select send.

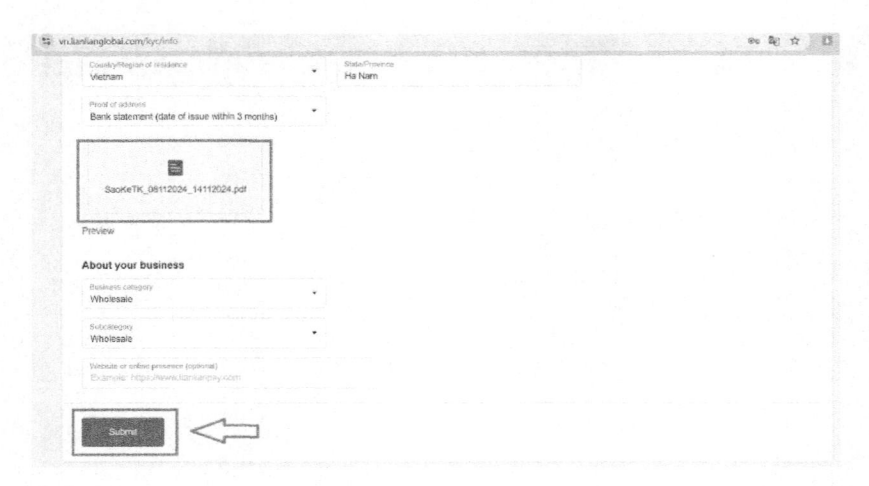

After selecting send and wait 1-3 days for Lian Lian global to confirm.

So we have successfully created a Lian Lian Global account.

CREATE AN AMAZON KDP ACCOUNT

Step 1: Access the website "kdp.amazon.com"

On the start page, select Join KDP

Step 2: Enter information: Full name, email address. After filling in, select "create your KDP account".

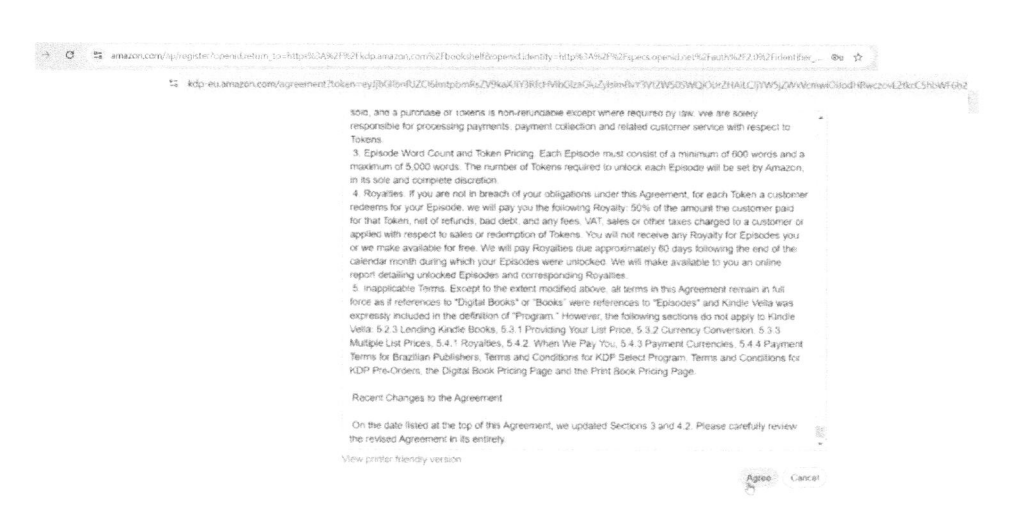

Receive OTP code to email and enter it.

Select Agree.

Step 3: On the home page, select your account.

Step 4: Enter your phone number and receive OTP.

Step5: In this section, we fill in personal information that matches the identity verification document.

When you have filled in all the required information, select save and continue.

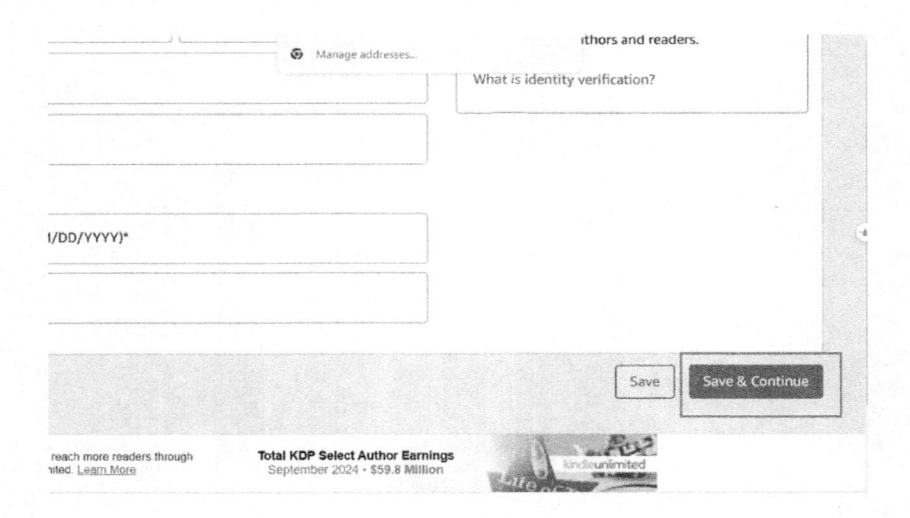

Step 6: In the 'Getting Paid' section, select the box to choose the location of your bank.

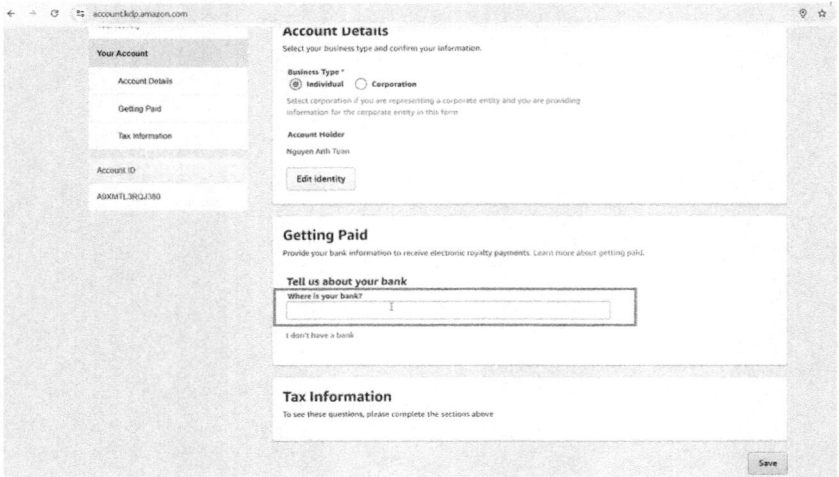

Step 7: We enter the last 9 characters of the account into routing number, account number into account number.

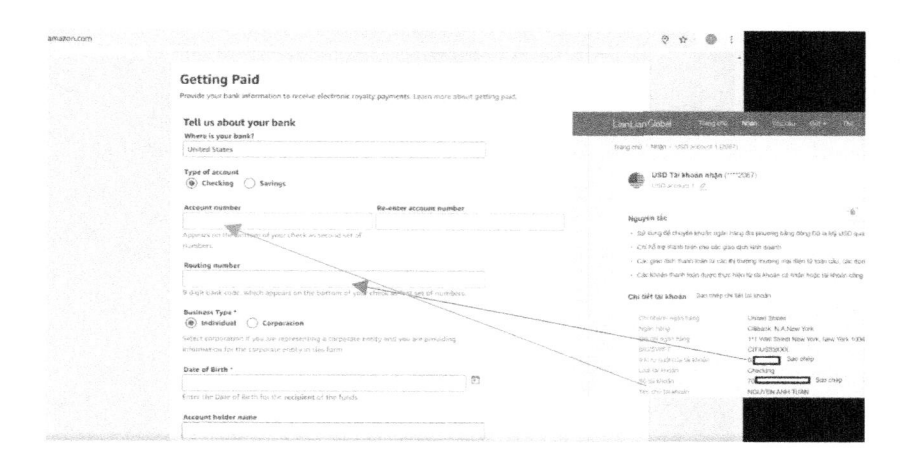

Step 8: Fill in other information that matches Lian Lian.

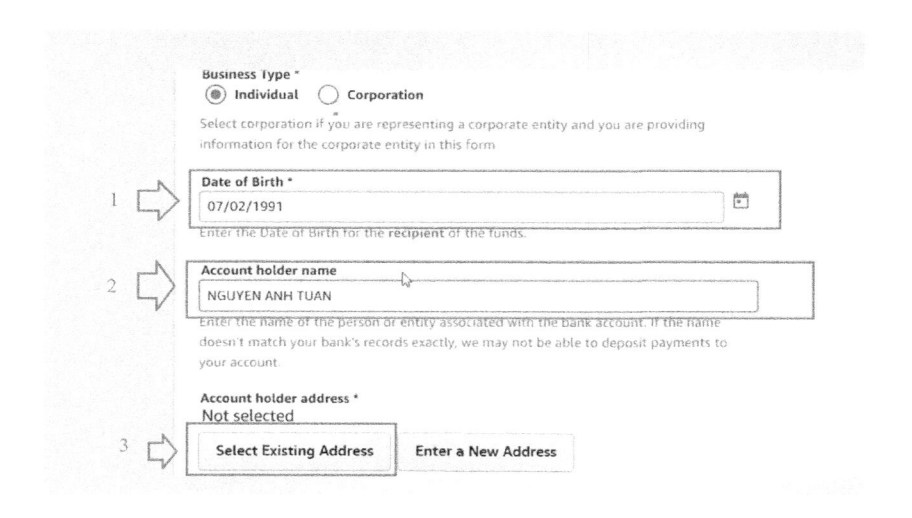

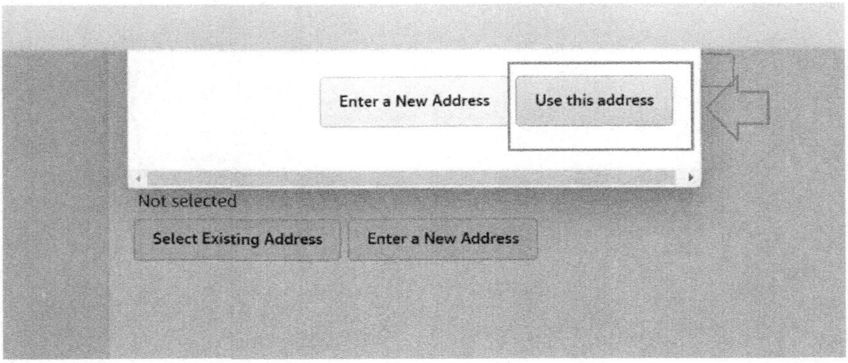
Enter a New Address
Use this address
Not selected
Select Existing Address
Enter a New Address

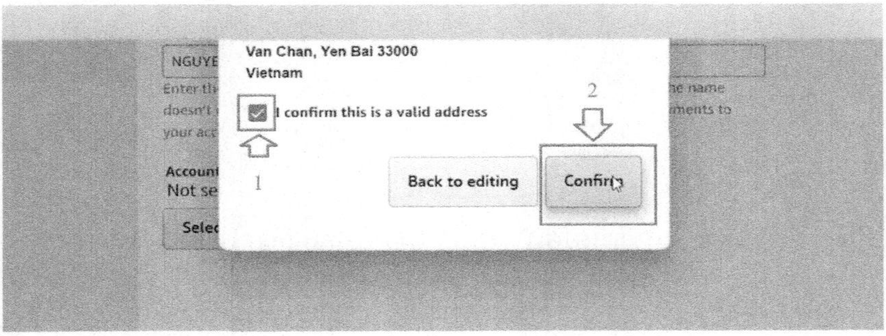
Van Chan, Yen Bai 33000
Vietnam
I confirm this is a valid address
1
2
Back to editing

Step 9: The next step involves the tax code: if a tax code is available, please provide the corresponding information. If no tax code exists, it can be disregarded, as this will not have an impact. For residents outside the United States, the system has already deducted the necessary amounts directly from royalties during sales made through the store.

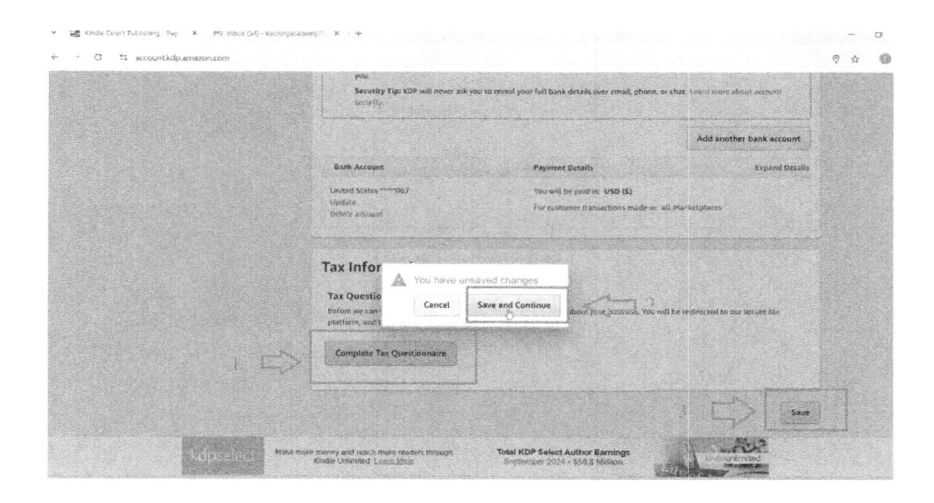

Upon completing the tax interview, we will proceed to the final step prior to publishing our books.

Step 10: Verify identity.

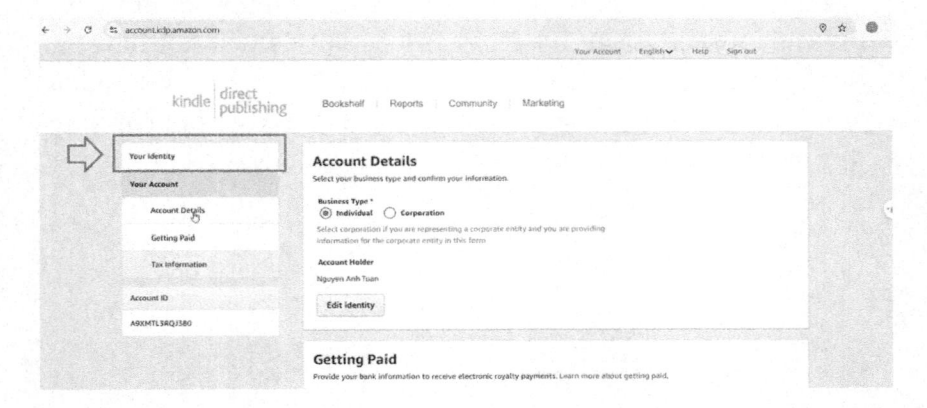

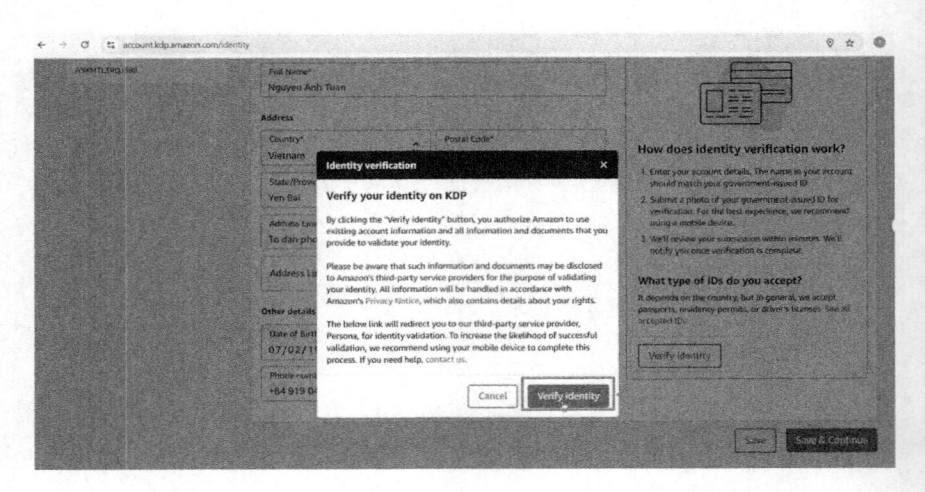

AI Publishing Profits

Please select the appropriate country and the documents we have prepared for your identity verification.

Select upload an image of your ID to upload a photo of the front and back of your ID, then select continue.

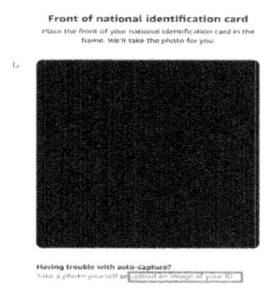

If you received the same message as above, we're excited to announce that you've successfully created and verified your account! Great job on reaching this important milestone. Now let's go publishing!

Chapter 3: Creating and Publishing with AI

Section 1: Using AI for Book Creation

Using AI to Create Bestseller Books: A Comprehensive Guide

Artificial Intelligence (AI) has transformed the publishing industry, enabling authors and creators to conceptualize, design, and publish books more efficiently than ever. However, the key to creating a bestseller isn't just leveraging AI—it's understanding how to strategically use these tools to craft unique, high-quality books that resonate with your target audience. In this guide, we'll explore, in detail, how to use AI to create a book that stands out in the competitive Amazon KDP marketplace.

1. Start with Research: Using AI to Identify Profitable Niches

Before you start writing, it's crucial to understand your market. AI tools can help you identify high-demand, low-competition niches that have the potential to become bestsellers.

Tools to Use:

- **ChatGPT:** Generate niche ideas and trends.

- **Publisher Rocket or BookBeam:** Analyze keywords, search volumes, and competition on Amazon.

- **Google Trends:** Track search trends for your niche.

How to Use These Tools:

Niche Brainstorming with ChatGPT:

Prompt: "What are some trending topics for self-help books in 2024?"

Example Response: Topics like mindfulness, digital detox, or overcoming imposter syndrome.

Keyword Analysis with Publisher Rocket:

Search for specific phrases like "mindfulness journal for beginners."

Identify keywords with high search volume but moderate competition.

Trends Analysis with Google Trends:

Enter your niche keywords and analyze their performance over time.

Example: Seasonal trends like "holiday stress relief coloring books."

Result: Choose a niche where demand is growing, competition is manageable, and audience needs are unmet.

2. Creating a Standout Concept with ChatGPT

Once you've identified your niche, use AI to refine your book's concept and structure.

How to Create a Unique Concept:

- Generate Book Titles:

Prompt: "Suggest creative titles for a journal about mindfulness."

☐ *Example Output: "Mindful Moments: A 30-Day Journey to Inner Peace."*

- Develop a Unique Angle:

☐ Use AI to brainstorm ways to differentiate your book.

☐ *Prompt: "How can a gratitude journal for teens stand out in the market?"*

☐ *Example Output: "Include relatable prompts based on teen challenges, such as social media pressures and academic stress."*

- Craft an Outline:

☐ Ask AI to draft a detailed outline based on your concept.

☐ *Prompt: "Create a 10-chapter outline for a self-help book on building self-confidence."*

Result: A well-defined concept and structure that aligns with market demand.

3. Writing the Manuscript with AI Assistance

AI can speed up the writing process without compromising quality. However, human input is essential for creativity and authenticity.

How to Write with AI:

- Draft Chapters:

☐ Use ChatGPT to generate initial drafts.

☐ *Prompt: "Write an introduction for a book about overcoming procrastination."*

- Enhance the Writing:

- Use AI tools like Grammarly or ProWritingAid for editing and refining.

- Focus on readability, grammar, and style consistency.

- Include Relatable Examples:

Prompt: "Provide real-life examples of overcoming procrastination for a self-help book."

Pro Tip: Break the writing into manageable chunks and provide specific prompts to guide AI responses.

4. Designing Covers and Illustrations with AI

The cover is the first thing potential readers see, and it plays a significant role in their decision to buy. AI tools like **MidJourney**, **Leonardo.ai**, and **Canva** make it easy to create professional-quality designs.

Steps for Creating a Bestseller-Worthy Cover:

- Generate Visuals with AI:

- Use MidJourney for unique illustrations.

- *Prompt: "A cozy winter cabin surrounded by snow, in watercolor style."*

- Design the Cover in Canva:

- Upload AI-generated visuals to Canva.

- Customize with fonts, colors, and layout that align with your niche.

- Example: Use calming colors and clean fonts for self-help books; bold, bright designs for children's books.

- Test Multiple Designs:

☐ Create variations and test them with friends or through social media polls to see which resonates most.

5. Enhancing Content with AI

AI isn't just for writing and design—it can also enhance the overall quality of your book by adding unique elements.

How to Enhance Your Book's Value:

- Interactive Elements:

☐ Use ChatGPT to create prompts, exercises, or interactive activities.

☐ Example: "Daily reflection prompts" for a journal or "creative challenges" for a coloring book.

- Incorporate Quotes and Inspirations:

☐ *Prompt: "Provide 10 motivational quotes about perseverance for a self-help book."*

- Localize Your Content:

☐ Tailor your book to specific audiences using AI.

☐ *Prompt: "Rewrite this passage to appeal to a US audience."*

6. Formatting and Preparing for Publishing

Formatting is a critical step in creating a professional-looking book. AI can streamline this process.

How to Format with AI and Tools:

- Use Atticus or Vellum for Formatting:

□ Upload your manuscript to these tools for automatic formatting.

　　□ Customize fonts, headers, and layouts for eBooks and print.

- AI for Consistency:

　　□ Use ChatGPT to create chapter summaries, back cover blurbs, or SEO-optimized descriptions.

- Test in the KDP Previewer:

　　□ Check your formatted manuscript in Amazon's previewer to ensure it looks great on all devices.

7. Automating the Marketing Process

AI can also help you promote your book effectively.

How to Use AI for Marketing:

- Create Ad Copy:

　　□ *Prompt: "Write a compelling Amazon ad copy for a coloring book for adults."*

- Social Media Content:

　　□ Use tools like **Pictory.ai** to create short promotional videos for Instagram or TikTok.

- Optimize Keywords:

　　□ Use Publisher Rocket to identify high-performing keywords for your book's title, subtitle, and description.

8. Real-Life Example: A Mindfulness Coloring Book

Scenario:

A creator wanted to publish a mindfulness coloring book for adults.

Steps Taken:

- Niche Research:

◻ Used Publisher Rocket to identify "mindfulness coloring books" as a high-demand, low-competition niche.

- Content Creation:

◻ Generated 50 mandala designs using MidJourney.

◻ Asked ChatGPT to write mindfulness tips for each design.

- Design and Formatting:

◻ Combined AI visuals and Canva for an eye-catching cover.

◻ Used Atticus to format for both eBook and print versions.

- Launch and Marketing:

◻ Promoted the book on Instagram using AI-generated videos and ads.

Result: The book ranked in the top 10 of its category within a month, earning over $3,000 in royalties in the first 30 days.

The AI Advantage

AI tools offer unparalleled advantages in speed, efficiency, and creativity. By combining the power of AI with your unique ideas and personal touch, you can create high-quality, engaging books that have the potential to become bestsellers. The secret is to use AI as an assistant, not a replacement, ensuring your books reflect originality and value.

AI as Your Co-Author

Gone are the days when creating a book meant spending months brainstorming ideas and crafting every word. With the advent of AI tools like ChatGPT, MidJourney, and Canva, you can streamline the book creation process, reduce costs, and elevate the quality of your work. In this section, we'll dive deep into how AI can assist you in generating ideas, developing content, and creating visually appealing designs.

Step 1: Generating Ideas and Outlines with AI

AI tools like **ChatGPT** are invaluable for brainstorming book ideas, creating detailed outlines, and even writing drafts. Here's how you can use AI for different types of books:

1. Brainstorming Book Ideas:

- Open ChatGPT and prompt it with questions like:

  "What are some trending topics for self-help books?"

  "Suggest unique themes for children's storybooks."

  "What niches are growing in popularity on Amazon KDP?"

- Use the results to identify profitable and engaging topics.

Example Output for "Low-Content Books":

ChatGPT may suggest ideas like:

- *"Daily Gratitude Journal with Prompts."*

- "*30-Day Fitness Planner with Progress Tracking.*"

2. Creating Detailed Outlines:

- Once you have a topic, ask ChatGPT to create a chapter-by-chapter breakdown.

   Prompt: "Outline a self-help book on overcoming procrastination in 10 chapters."

- Refine the outline by adding personal touches or specific themes relevant to your audience.

3. Writing Content:

- Use ChatGPT to draft sections of your book.

   Prompt: "Write a 500-word introduction for a mindfulness coloring book."

- Edit and customize the AI-generated content to ensure it aligns with your style and tone.

Pro Tip: Always add a human touch to AI-written content. This ensures authenticity and emotional resonance with readers.

Step 2: Creating Illustrations and Designs

AI-generated visuals are transforming the way books are designed. Tools like **MidJourney** and **Leonardo.ai** allow you to create stunning illustrations, while **Canva** simplifies the design process.

1. Using MidJourney for Illustrations:

- MidJourney specializes in generating intricate and unique visuals.

- *Example:* For a fantasy storybook, prompt MidJourney with:

    "*A magical forest with glowing trees and mythical creatures, in watercolor style.*"

- Use the AI-generated illustrations as your book's interior artwork or cover elements.

2. Creating Covers with Canva:

- Canva is ideal for designing professional-looking book covers, even if you have no prior experience.
- Use Canva's templates and customize them to fit your niche.
- *Example:*
    - For a self-help journal: Use minimalist designs with calming colors.
    - For a children's storybook: Add bold, vibrant illustrations with playful fonts.

3. Combining Tools for a Polished Look:

- Use AI-generated visuals from MidJourney or Leonardo.ai and refine them in Canva for a cohesive design.
- *Workflow:* Generate artwork → Export → Upload to Canva → Add text and finishing touches.

Step 3: Examples of High-Profit Book Types

1. Low-Content Books:

- Examples: Journals, planners, and coloring books.

- Why They Work: Easy to produce and evergreen demand.

2. Storybooks for Kids:

- Examples: Picture books for ages 3–5, illustrated adventure stories for ages 6–8.
- Why They Work: Parents and educators constantly seek engaging stories for children.

3. Adult Coloring Books:

- Examples: Mandalas for relaxation, inspirational quote coloring books.
- Why They Work: Popular for stress relief and mindfulness.

4. Informational eBooks:

- Examples: Guides on personal finance, health, or productivity.
- Why They Work: eBooks are lightweight, low-cost, and highly scalable.

Step 4: Automating Content Creation

AI also excels at automating repetitive tasks, saving you valuable time.

1. Templates for Journals and Planners:

- Use tools like Canva or BookBolt to create templates for journals and planners.

- Add AI-generated prompts or themes to make your book stand out.

2. Streamlining Revisions with AI:

- Use **Grammarly** or **ProWritingAid** to refine and polish your manuscript.

- Use ChatGPT for restructuring sentences or improving clarity.

   Prompt: "Rewrite this paragraph to make it more engaging."

Step 5: Ensuring Originality and Quality

AI is a tool, not a replacement for originality. Always review and enhance AI-generated content to make it uniquely yours.

Tips for Maintaining Quality:

1. Cross-check AI-generated ideas and content with market trends.

2. Add your voice and expertise to differentiate your work.

3. Use plagiarism checkers to ensure originality (e.g., Copyscape or Grammarly Premium).

AI as Your Creative Partner

Using AI for book creation allows you to focus on creativity and strategy while reducing time spent on repetitive tasks. By leveraging tools like ChatGPT, MidJourney, and Canva, you can produce high-quality, engaging books that resonate with your audience. With AI as your co-author, the possibilities are endless.

Section 2: Designing Irresistible Book Covers

Why Your Book Cover Matters

Your book cover is the first impression readers get of your work. On Amazon, where countless books compete for attention, an eye-catching and professional cover can be the deciding factor between a click and a scroll past. This section focuses on creating irresistible book covers using AI tools and design principles to captivate your target audience.

1. The Psychology of Book Covers

Understanding the psychology behind what makes a cover appealing is essential for designing one that converts viewers into buyers.

Key Elements to Focus On:

- Color Palette:

  ☐ Calming blues and greens for self-help and mindfulness books.

  ☐ Bright, playful colors for children's books.

  ☐ Dark tones with bold contrasts for thrillers or mysteries.

- Typography:

  ☐ Choose fonts that reflect the book's theme.

  ☐ Example: Elegant serif fonts for romance, bold sans-serif fonts for non-fiction.

- Imagery:

- Illustrations or photos should evoke emotion and curiosity.
- Avoid clutter; less is often more.

2. Choosing the Right AI Tools for Cover Design

AI tools simplify the design process, enabling you to create professional-quality covers even without graphic design experience.

Recommended Tools:

- MidJourney or Leonardo.ai:

- Generate unique, high-quality illustrations and backgrounds.
- *Example:* For a fantasy novel, prompt MidJourney with:
  - *"A mystical forest with glowing mushrooms and magical creatures, in vibrant colors."*

- Canva:

- Combine AI-generated visuals with Canva's templates to add text and design elements.
- Ideal for adding titles, subtitles, and author names in cohesive layouts.

- Adobe Express or GIMP (Free Alternative):

- For advanced users, these tools allow for greater customization of AI-generated designs.

3. Steps to Design an Irresistible Cover

Step 1: Define Your Audience

Understand who your readers are and what appeals to them.

- *Example:* For a mindfulness journal, your audience might prefer minimalistic, clean designs with calming colors.

Step 2: Create a Rough Concept

Use ChatGPT to brainstorm cover ideas.

- *Prompt:* "What elements should a cover for a self-help book include?"
- Example Response:
  - Keywords: Minimalist, uplifting imagery, soft color gradients.

Step 3: Generate Visuals with AI

1. Use MidJourney to create a background or central image.
   - *Prompt:* "A peaceful sunset over a calm ocean, digital painting style."
2. Save the generated artwork and prepare it for further editing.

Step 4: Add Text in Canva

1. Choose a clean, professional font.
2. Add the book's title, subtitle, and author name.
3. Experiment with placement to ensure readability and balance.

Step 5: Export and Review

1. Export the cover in the correct dimensions for Amazon KDP:

eBook: 1600 x 2560 pixels.

Paperback: Adjust for trim size and spine width (e.g., 6 x 9 inches).

2. Use Amazon's Cover Creator tool or previewer to verify how it appears on various devices.

4. Tips for a Professional Finish

- Stick to Your Genre Standards:

Each genre has specific design trends. Study top-selling books in your category to understand what works.

- Test Variations:

Create 2–3 versions of your cover and test them with friends, social media followers, or through polling tools like PollMaker.

- Avoid Common Mistakes:

- Overcrowded designs with too many elements.
- Hard-to-read fonts.
- Poor image resolution or pixelation.

5. Real-Life Example: A Children's Book Cover

Scenario:
You're publishing a children's storybook about a brave rabbit named Benny.

Steps Taken:

- Concept:

Used ChatGPT to brainstorm ideas:

- *"A playful rabbit standing in a meadow under a rainbow."*

- Illustration:

- Generated artwork in MidJourney using the prompt:

  - *"A cheerful cartoon rabbit in a vibrant meadow, watercolor style."*

- Design:

- Combined the illustration with playful fonts in Canva.
- Used bold, bright colors to appeal to kids and parents.

Result: A visually engaging cover that clearly communicates the book's theme and target audience.

6. Enhancing Covers with Special Features

- Add Subtle Textures or Patterns:

- Use overlays in Canva or Adobe Express to add depth and sophistication.

- Highlight Awards or Endorsements:

- Add badges like "#1 New Release" or quotes from reviews.

- Create 3D Mockups:

- Use tools like **BookBrush** or **DIYBookCovers.com** to create 3D renders for marketing materials.

7. Leveraging AI for Continuous Improvement

AI isn't just for initial design—it can help refine and adapt your covers over time.

- Use ChatGPT to suggest alternative taglines or subtitles.
- Experiment with new visuals in MidJourney to refresh the design for second editions.

Designing a Bestseller-Worthy Cover

Your cover is your book's first ambassador. With AI tools and a solid understanding of design principles, you can create covers that grab attention, reflect your book's essence, and convert views into sales. By testing and refining, you'll ensure your cover is always optimized for success.

INSTRUCTIONS FOR CREATING A COMPLETE COLORING BOOK

Create the content of the book body and cover

Step 1: Access the website "chatGPT.com"

Step 2: Enter required input data (subject, description, number of pages,...)

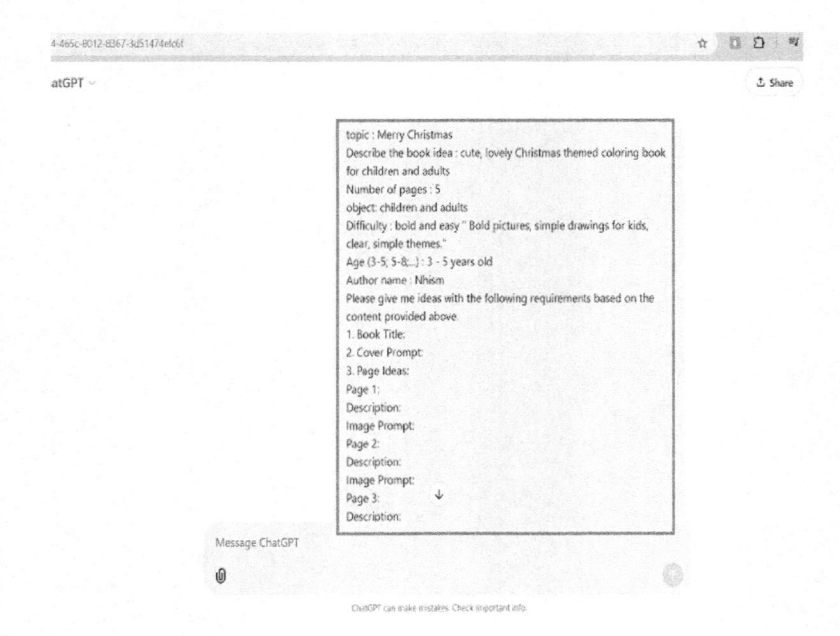

AI will provide ideas and content that match the given requirements.

ChatGPT

1. Book Title:

My Merry Christmas Coloring Book

2. Cover Prompt:

A festive, vibrant cover featuring a cheerful Santa Claus holding a gift bag, surrounded by adorable reindeer, a decorated Christmas tree, and snowflakes. The title is bold and playful, with candy cane stripes. In the background, soft snow is falling, creating a magical Christmas vibe. The author's name, Whizm, is placed neatly at the bottom in a whimsical font.

3. Page Ideas:

Page 1:

Description:
A joyful Santa Claus waving while standing next to his sleigh filled with presents.

Image Prompt:
Santa is dressed in his iconic red suit, waving with one hand while the other rests on a sleigh brimming with oversized, wrapped gifts. A simple, bold design with a snowy background and a clear sky.

Create book cover and book page images.

Create book cover image

At the chatGPT interface after creating content.

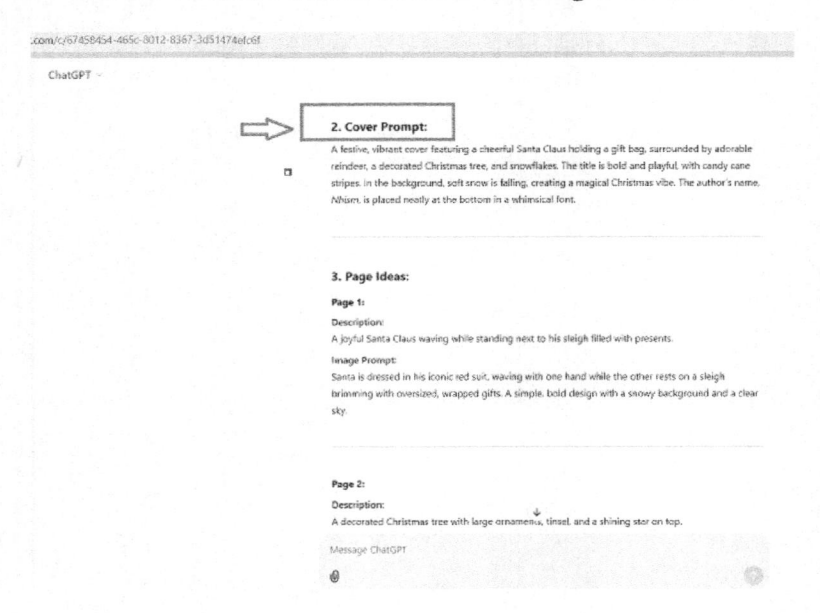

Step1: Copy the content in the "cover prompt" section.

Step2: Access professional photo creation websites.

For example: "app.leonardo.ai", "ideogram.ai",...

On Leonardo's home page, select image creation.

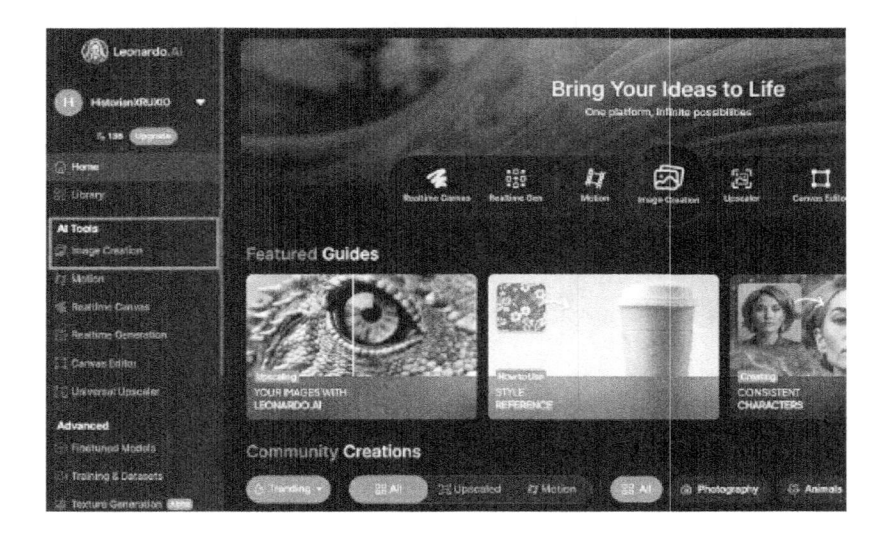

Then paste the copied content in the cover prompt into the search bar and press generate.

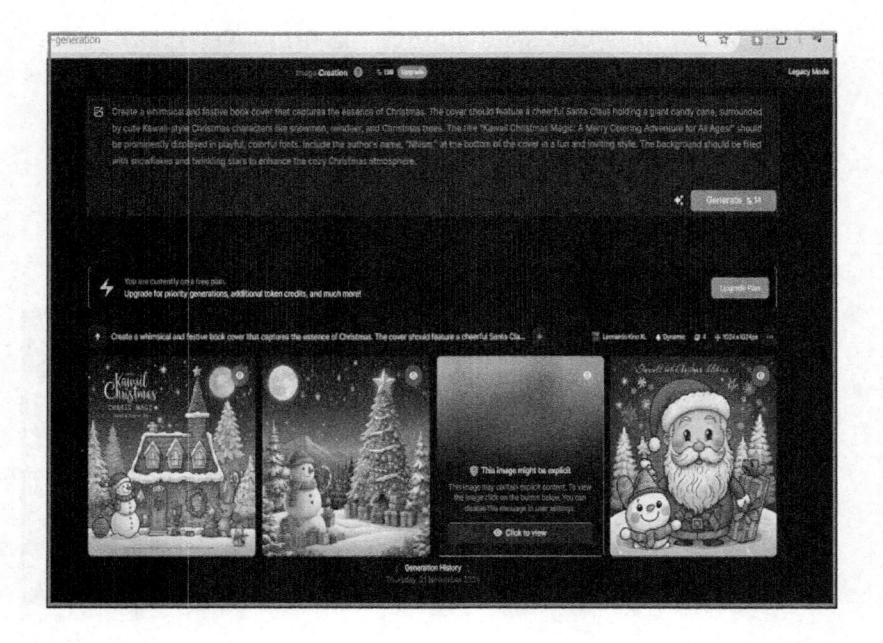

After selecting a satisfactory photo, save the file to your computer.

Create coloring book pages for the book content (black and white outlines)

At the chat page, GPT will provide us with ideas for creating photos 'Image Prompt':

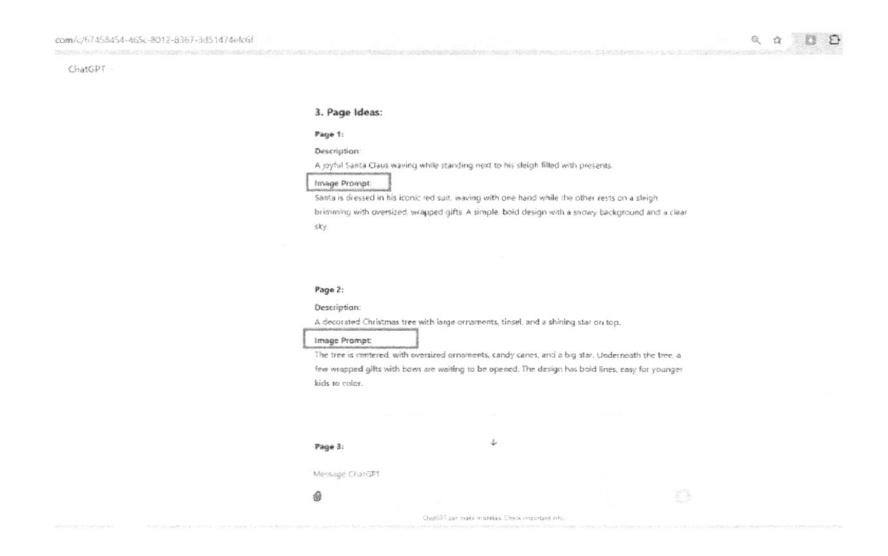

Tony Trieu

Step1: Copy the content in the image prompt:

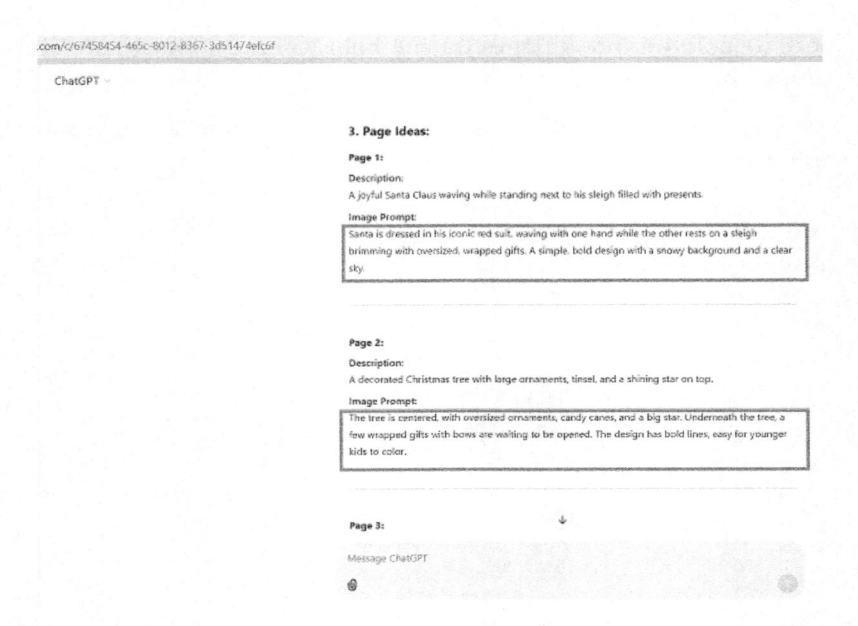

Step2: Visit professional photo creation websites.

Some free sites to consider:

"https://ideogram.ai/";

"https://chat.openai.com/";

"https://designer.microsoft.com/",

Paste the copied prompt and hit Enter:

After selecting a satisfactory image, save the file to your computer.

Continue to create at least 36 images to suit the requirements of the coloring book.

Create book cover files and manuscript files.

Create the book cover file:

Step 1: Utilize any design application to create a book cover file that meets Amazon's specifications. In this tutorial, we will use Canva to edit the book files.

Upload all the coloring book pages to Canva, ensuring that each photo is separated by a blank page. The total number of pages in the manuscript must be 24 or more to meet Amazon KDP requirements.

Step 2: Adjust the margins to fit the book pages properly.

Once you have completed the editing, save the file as a PDF.

Create the book cover file

Step 1: Visit the website "https://kdp.amazon.com/cover-calculator" to get a cover sample file with the correct size of the number of pages you provided:

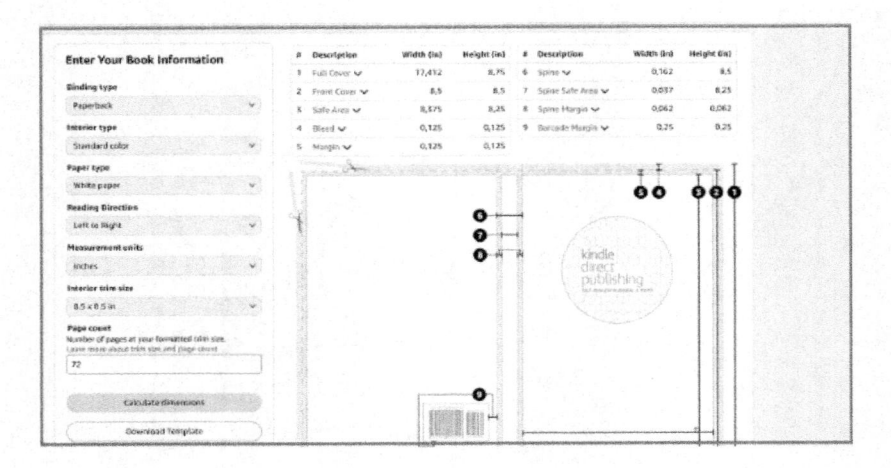

Once you have the book cover information, proceed to download the template.

Step 2: Upload the template file to canva and start editing.

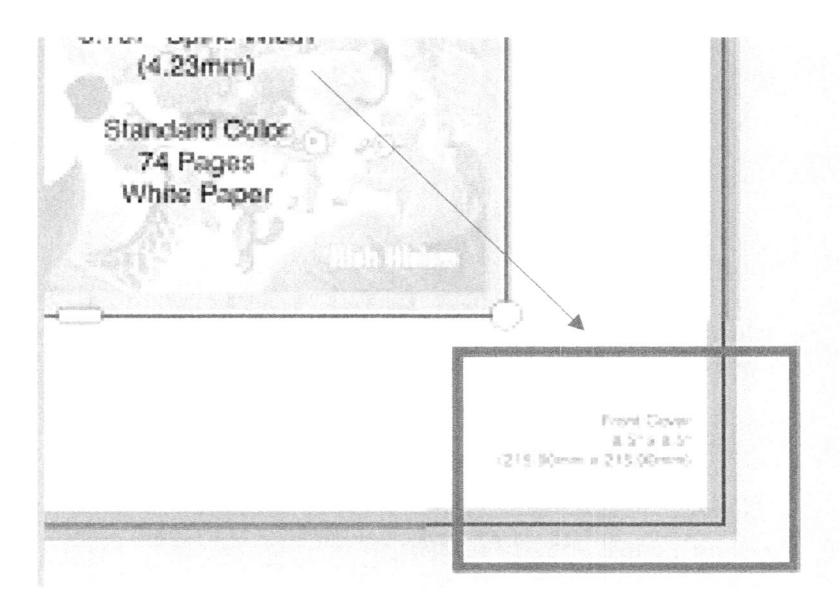

Note: Align the front and back cover images so that they cover the pink part of the template file.

Tips: lower the opacity for easier alignment.

After editing, save the file as PDF.

SO WE HAVE SUCCESSFULLY CREATED A COLORING BOOK!

HOW TO CONSISTENT CHARACTER FOR STORY BOOK
Step 1: Generate story ideas
Use Chat GPT to create a story.

Ask ChatGPT to create an image prompt for each scene.

Ask ChatGPT to create an image prompt for the cover book.

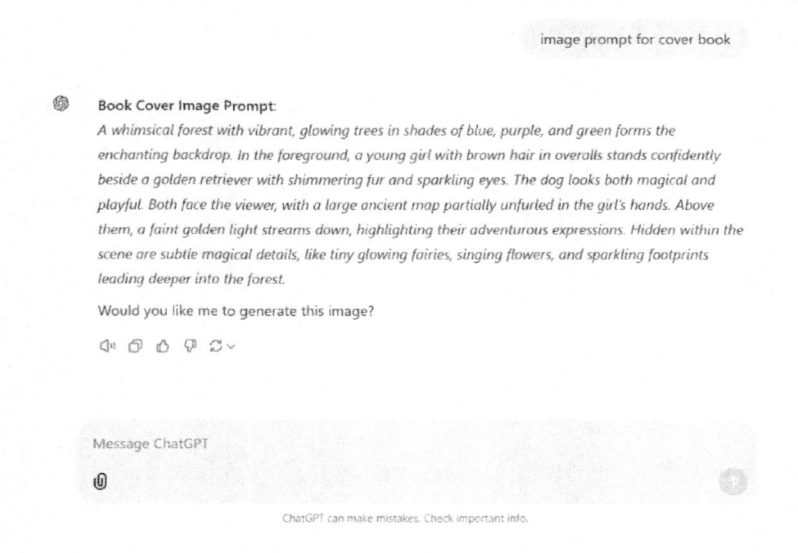

> image prompt for cover book

Book Cover Image Prompt:
A whimsical forest with vibrant, glowing trees in shades of blue, purple, and green forms the enchanting backdrop. In the foreground, a young girl with brown hair in overalls stands confidently beside a golden retriever with shimmering fur and sparkling eyes. The dog looks both magical and playful. Both face the viewer, with a large ancient map partially unfurled in the girl's hands. Above them, a faint golden light streams down, highlighting their adventurous expressions. Hidden within the scene are subtle magical details, like tiny glowing fairies, singing flowers, and sparkling footprints leading deeper into the forest.

Would you like me to generate this image?

Step 2: Use Canva to create a consistent character design. Open Canva and select 'Create a design' → 'Custom size.' Set the dimensions based on your desired page size, then click 'Create new design.'

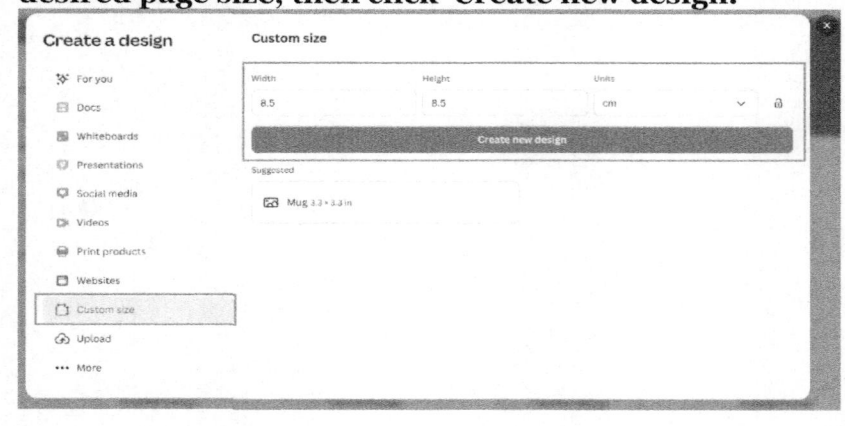

Use **Magic Media** tool to generate images.

Paste each Prompt of each scene book from ChatGPT into the description box.

Tips: *Components should be in one prompt to consistent character creations:*

> "Seed number: 435678, [character description] [activity of character], consistent character"

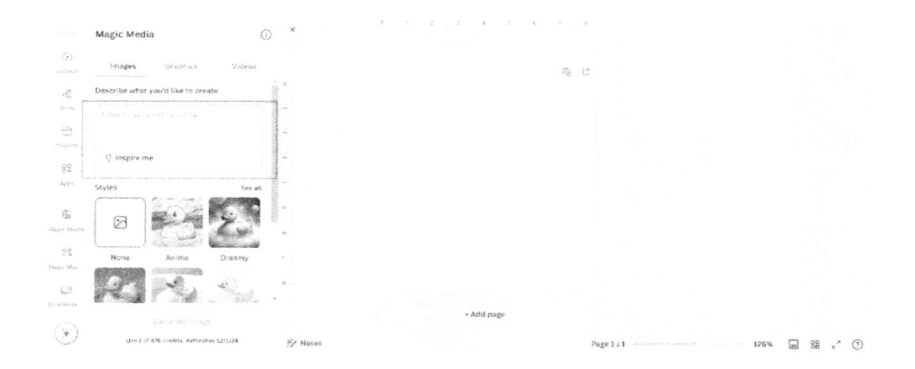

Choose style you want for the book.

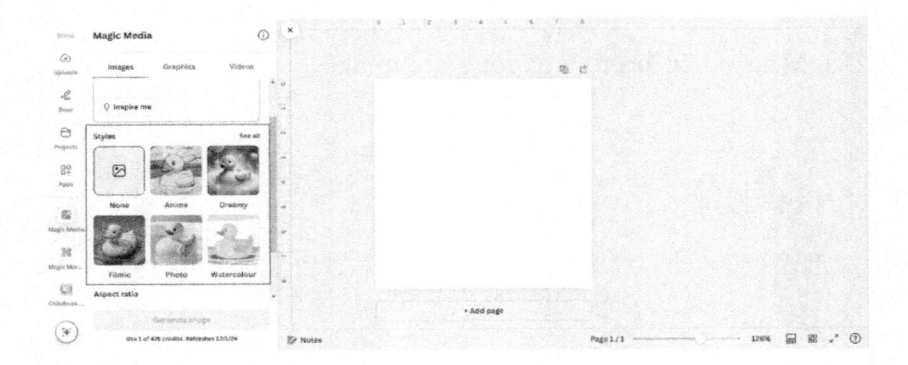

For example:

> "**Seed number: 435678,** [Emma, A young girl with messy brown hair, wearing brown overalls and sneakers], [walks beside a golden retriever that glows faintly, both gazing at a large stone tablet with an ancient map carved into it], **consistent character.**"

After the new image is created, click **Generate more like this** to create more images you want with the exact character you created. Or click **Generate again** to recreate another image if you are not satisfied.

To generate the next image, simply edit the sample prompt, keep the character description the same, change the character's action, and click **Generate again**. Click **Add page** to add page book.

Resize the photo to match the size of the existing frame.

You can add more text or elements to each page to make it more interesting.

Keep doing this until you have completed your book.

Step 3: Finish the book
Once you have created all the pages, click **Share** → **Download**.

Select the format you want (PNG or PDF) for the book and click **Download** to complete.

That's all. *Good luck with your book publishing!*

Section 3: Formatting and Uploading to KDP

The Importance of Formatting

Proper formatting is the backbone of a professional-looking book. It ensures that your text, images, and layout appear correctly on e-readers, print editions, and all other platforms where your book will be published. In this section, we'll guide you step by step on how to format your manuscript and upload it seamlessly to Amazon KDP.

Preparing Your Manuscript for Formatting

- Choose the Right Format for Your Book:

- **eBook (Kindle):** For digital readers, your manuscript should be in a format compatible with Kindle devices, such as EPUB or MOBI.

- **Paperback and Hardcover:** Requires PDF files with precise margins and bleed settings.

- Clean Up Your Manuscript:

- Use a consistent font style and size (e.g., Times New Roman, 12pt).
- Ensure proper alignment, paragraph spacing, and indentation.
- Remove extra line breaks or spaces.

- Tools to Use:

- **Microsoft Word:** Ideal for creating clean, formatted text files.
- **Google Docs:** Free alternative for basic formatting.
- **Scrivener or Atticus:** Advanced tools designed specifically for book authors.

2. Formatting for eBooks

Amazon KDP's eBooks require specific formatting for Kindle devices.

Steps to Format for Kindle:

-Layout Setup:

- Use single spacing for text.
- Insert page breaks between chapters.
- Ensure images are high-resolution (at least 300 DPI) and properly anchored.

-Create a Table of Contents:

- Use heading styles (e.g., Heading 1 for chapter titles) so that Kindle devices automatically generate a clickable table of contents.

- Export Your Manuscript:

- Save the file as a Word document (.docx) or convert it to EPUB using tools like **Calibre** or **Atticus**.

3. Formatting for Print (Paperback and Hardcover)

Print formatting requires precise specifications to ensure your book looks professional when printed.

-Set Trim Size:

- Choose your book size (e.g., 6 x 9 inches, 5.5 x 8.5 inches).
- Amazon provides templates for different trim sizes; download one that matches your choice.

- Adjust Margins and Bleed:

- Margins should accommodate for print binding (usually 0.5–1 inch).
- Include a 0.125-inch bleed if your book has images extending to the edge.

- Add Page Numbers and Headers:

- Insert page numbers starting from Chapter 1 (skip numbering the title page).
- Add headers with the book's title and your name.

- Export as PDF:

- Use "Save As" or "Export" in Word or Google Docs to generate a print-ready PDF.
- Ensure images are high-resolution to avoid pixelation.

4. Tools for Professional Formatting

- Atticus:

- A powerful, user-friendly tool for formatting both eBooks and print books.
- Provides templates and automation for chapter layouts, margins, and fonts.

- Vellum:

- Ideal for Mac users, offering drag-and-drop functionality and polished templates.

- Canva for Layouts:

- Use Canva to design custom interiors for low-content books like journals or planners.

- Adobe InDesign:

- Professional-grade software for advanced layout design.

5. Uploading Your Book to Amazon KDP

Once your manuscript is formatted, you're ready to upload it to Amazon KDP.

- Log into Your KDP Account:

- Navigate to your **Bookshelf** and click **+ Add New Title**.

- Enter Book Details:

- **Book Title and Subtitle:** Use SEO-optimized keywords.
- **Description:** Write a compelling synopsis for potential buyers.
- **Categories:** Select up to two categories relevant to your book's genre.

- Upload Your Manuscript:

- eBooks: Upload your .docx or EPUB file.
- Print Books: Upload your PDF.

- Upload Your Cover:

- Use the Amazon Cover Creator tool or upload a custom-designed cover (PDF or JPEG).

- Preview Your Book:

- Use the KDP Previewer to check for formatting errors or visual inconsistencies.

- Set Pricing and Distribution:

- Choose a royalty option (35% or 70% for eBooks).
- Set pricing for global markets.

6. Common Formatting and Uploading Issues

- File Rejections:

- Ensure your file size doesn't exceed Amazon's limits.
- Check for unsupported fonts or images.

- Formatting Errors:

- Fix alignment or margin issues using the KDP Previewer.
- Use Amazon's formatting guidelines for precise specifications.

- Metadata Mistakes:

- Double-check your title, author name, and categories to ensure they align with your book's content.

7. Real-Life Example: Formatting a Self-Help Journal

Scenario: A creator wanted to publish a mindfulness journal with inspirational quotes and writing prompts.

Steps Taken:

- Manuscript Preparation:

☐ Used Google Docs to create a simple layout with headers for each day's prompts.

☐ Added inspirational quotes sourced from public domain content.

- Formatting:

☐ Exported the manuscript to Atticus for final formatting and PDF generation.

☐ Used Canva to design the interior pages, incorporating subtle floral patterns.

- Upload:

☐ Uploaded the PDF to KDP, previewed it for consistency, and adjusted margins based on the preview.

Result:

The journal launched smoothly and received praise for its professional design and ease of use.

Formatting and uploading may seem like technical steps, but they're critical for presenting your book professionally. With the right tools and attention to detail, you can create a seamless reading experience that enhances your book's appeal and boosts sales. Proper formatting shows readers that you care about quality, setting the stage for a successful publishing journey.

INSTRUCTIONS ON HOW TO PUBLISH BOOKS ON AMAZON

Step 1: On the home page, select "Create"

Or 'Create a book'.

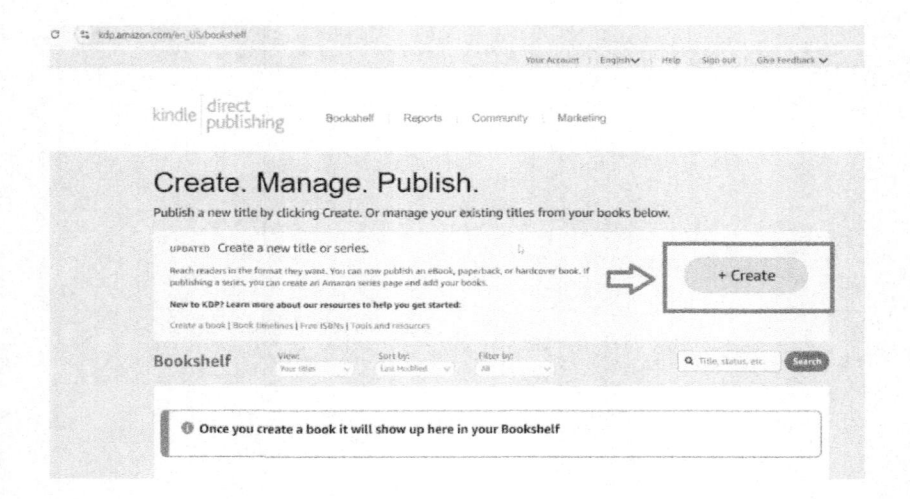

Step 2: Amazon offers a wide variety of books, including Kindle eBooks, paperbacks, hardcovers, and series collections.

In this guide, we will focus on the paperback genre, which is suitable for many different types of books.

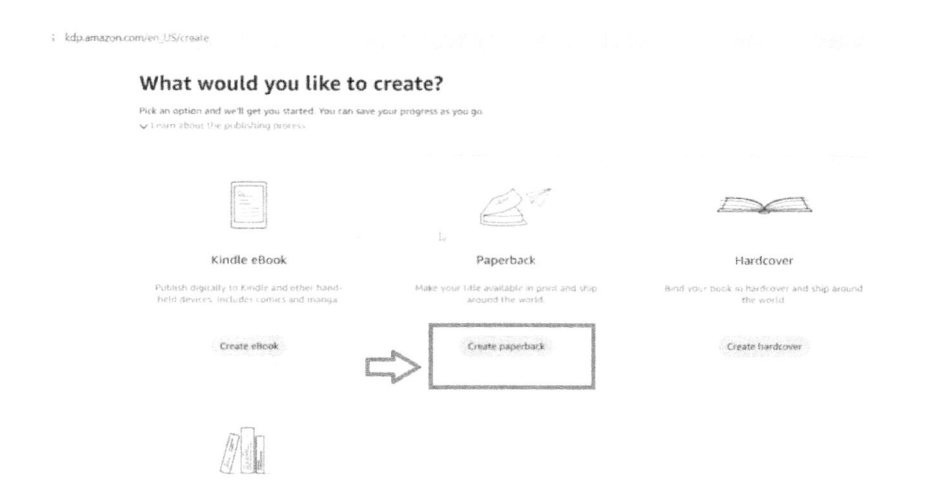

Step 3: Start with book title and subtitle.

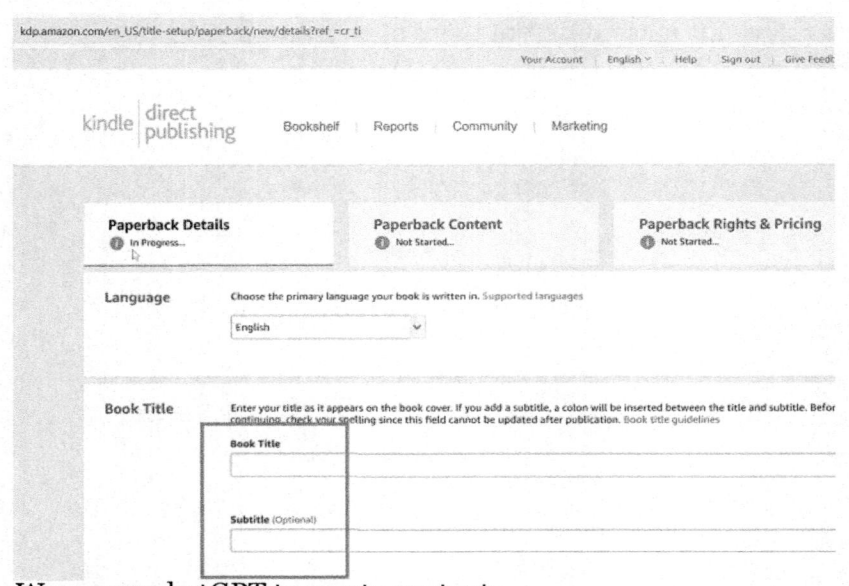

We access chatGPT to create content.

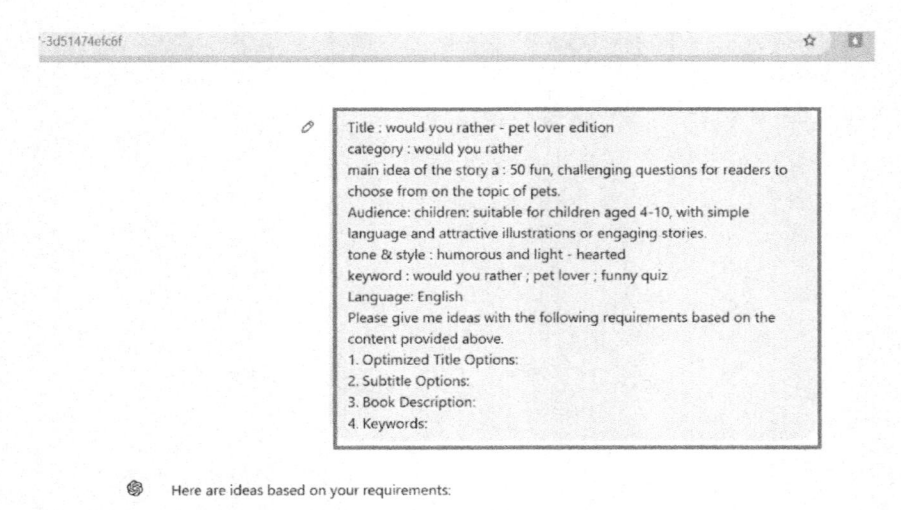

Title : would you rather - pet lover edition
category : would you rather
main idea of the story a : 50 fun, challenging questions for readers to choose from on the topic of pets.
Audience: children: suitable for children aged 4-10, with simple language and attractive illustrations or engaging stories.
tone & style : humorous and light - hearted
keyword : would you rather ; pet lover ; funny quiz
Language: English
Please give me ideas with the following requirements based on the content provided above.
1. Optimized Title Options:
2. Subtitle Options:
3. Book Description:
4. Keywords:

Here are ideas based on your requirements:

After entering the required data, chatGPT will give us the necessary content.

ChatGPT

1. Optimized Title Options

1. Would You Rather? Pet Lover's Edition
2. Furry Friends Dilemma: A Pet Lover's Would You Rather
3. Giggles & Paws: Would You Rather for Pet Fans
4. Would You Rather: Purrs, Woofs, and Laughs!
5. Pet-Tastic Choices: Would You Rather for Kids

2. Subtitle Options

1. 50 Funny and Challenging Questions for Young Pet Fans
2. A Whimsical Quiz for Kids Who Love Animals
3. Playful Questions to Keep Kids Laughing and Guessing
4. The Ultimate Quiz for Animal-Loving Kids (Ages 4-10)
5. Laugh, Imagine, Choose: A Pet Quiz Adventure

Step 4: In the book title section, note: the book title cover in your cover file must match the title.

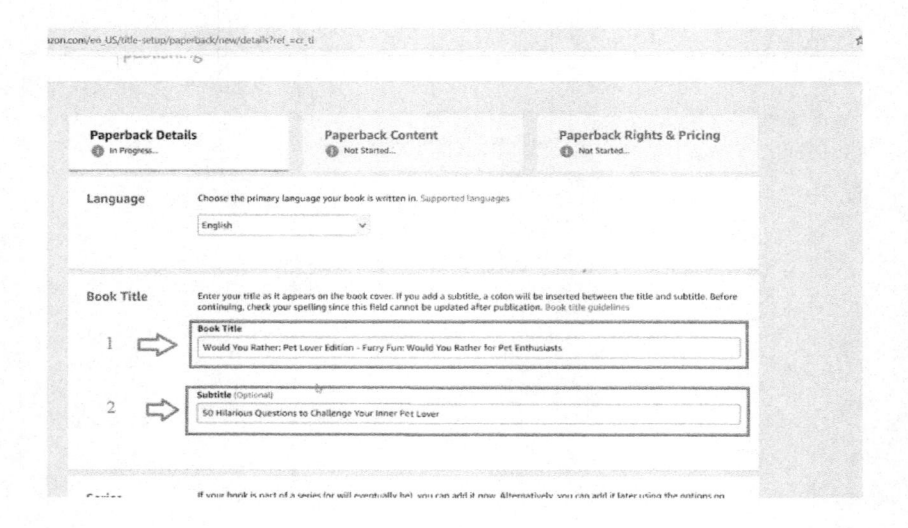

Step 5: If the book has multiple related parts, we will create additional series. Since this is the first book, we can skip this step for now. The edition number indicates how many times the book has been reprinted. After a successful publication, Amazon allows us to edit the content of the book. For the initial publication, we can also skip this part.

Step 6: Next is the 'Author' section, which refers to the author name. Here, each book can have one author name, although we recommend using just one for consistency. In the contributors section, you can include up to nine author names if the book has multiple authors.

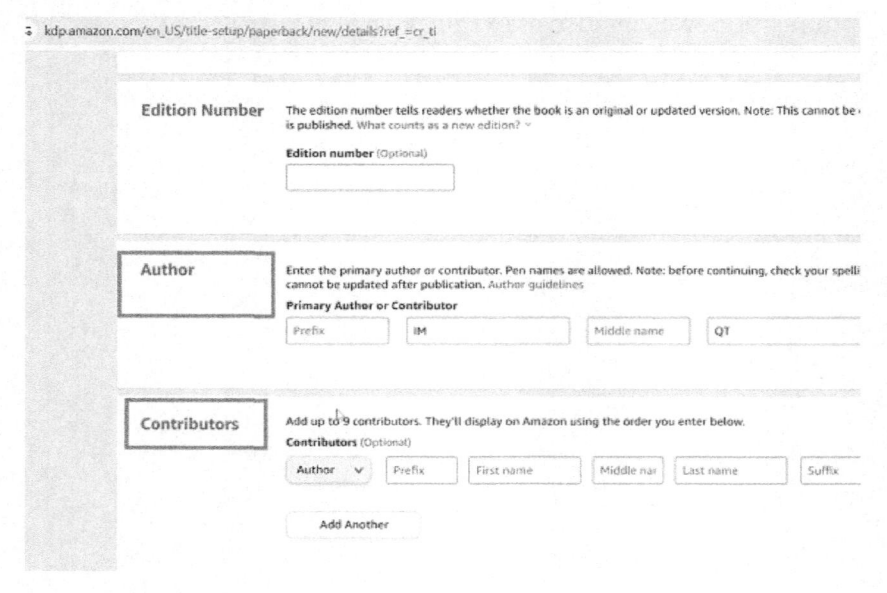

Step 7 : Description is the content of the description we can get from chatGPT. Get from the book description section until before the keywords section.

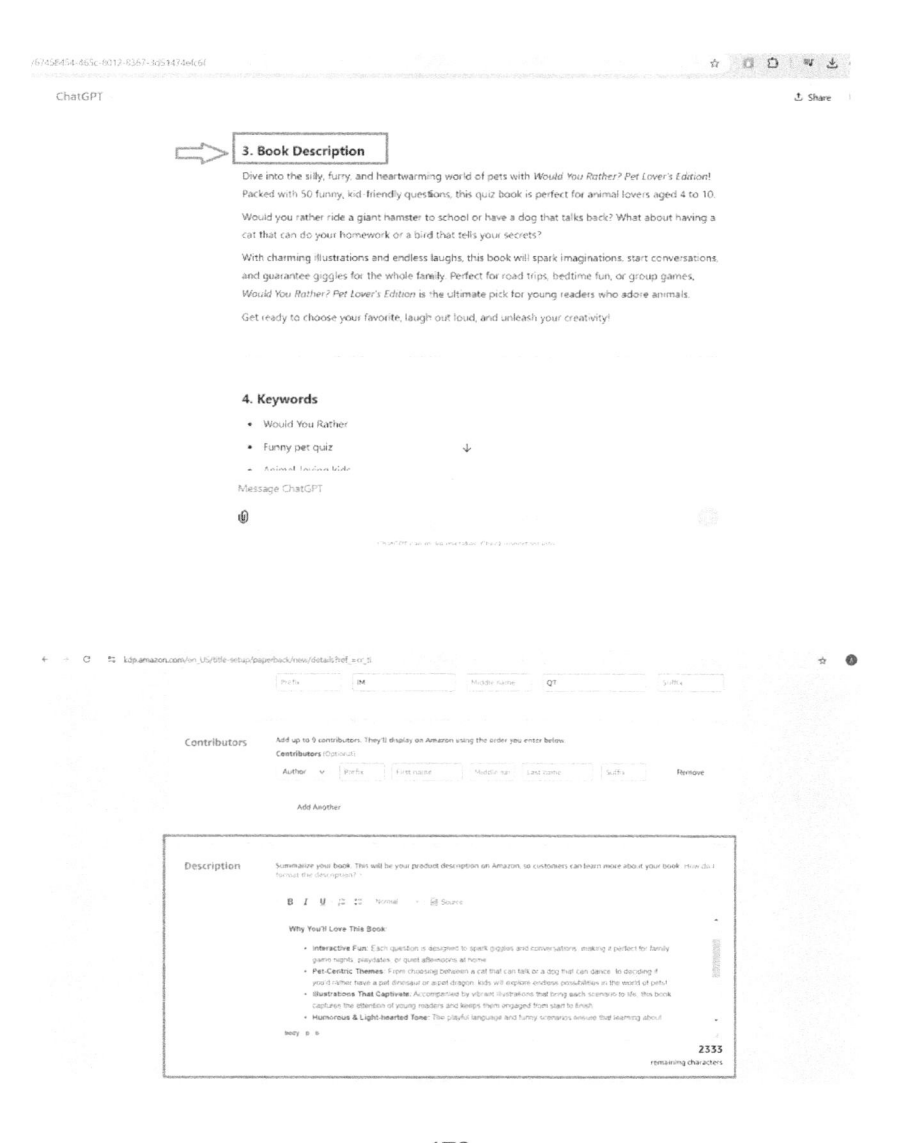

Step 8 : Publishing Rights (copyright) we choose the above option. In the Primary Audience section, with the question of whether the title and image contain sensitive content, we choose No. Reading age (reading age from smallest to largest) can be ignored or set to the smallest or largest.

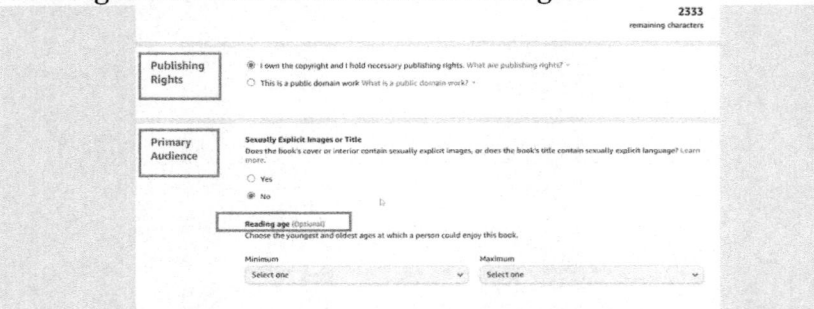

Step 9 : Primary marketplace (market) we can choose amazon.com

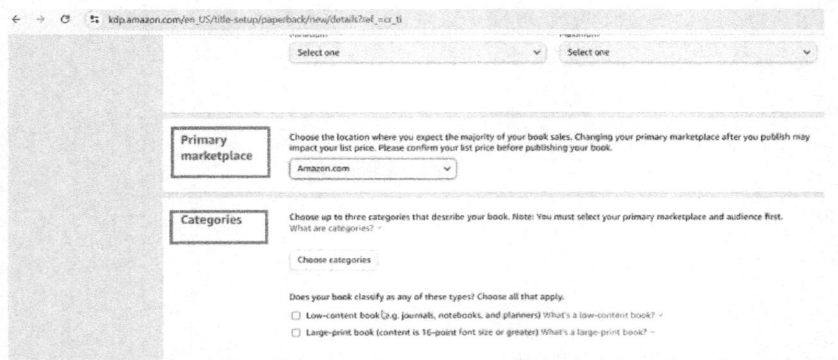

Explore categories from other top-selling titles in the book publishing niche: this section allows for manual selection.

Step 10 : For keywords, we can go to chatGPT to get the most relevant suggested terms. Or we can fill in the related words ourselves.

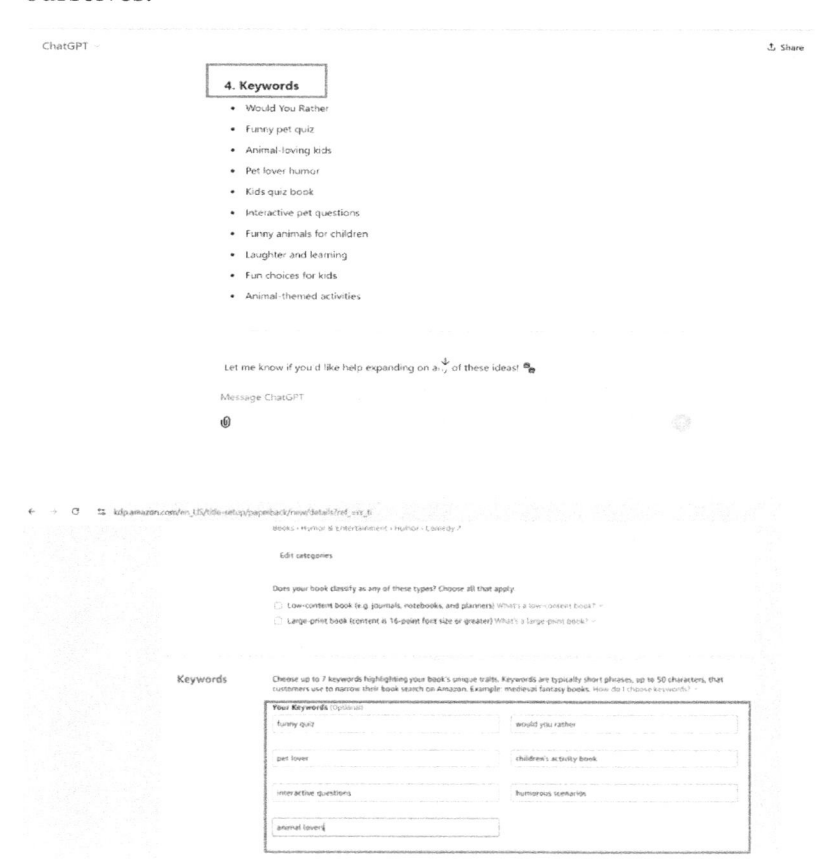

Step 11: Publication Date: If your book is complete, you can leave this as the default. The Release Date is the one you can edit. After making your selections, click "Save and Continue."

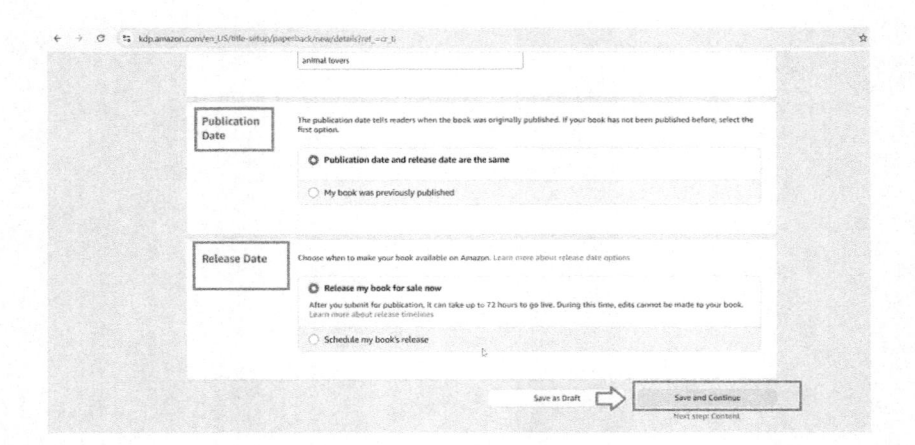

Step 12 : At the paperback Content interface

ISBN: 1 national and international standard identification number, we choose Assign ISBN.

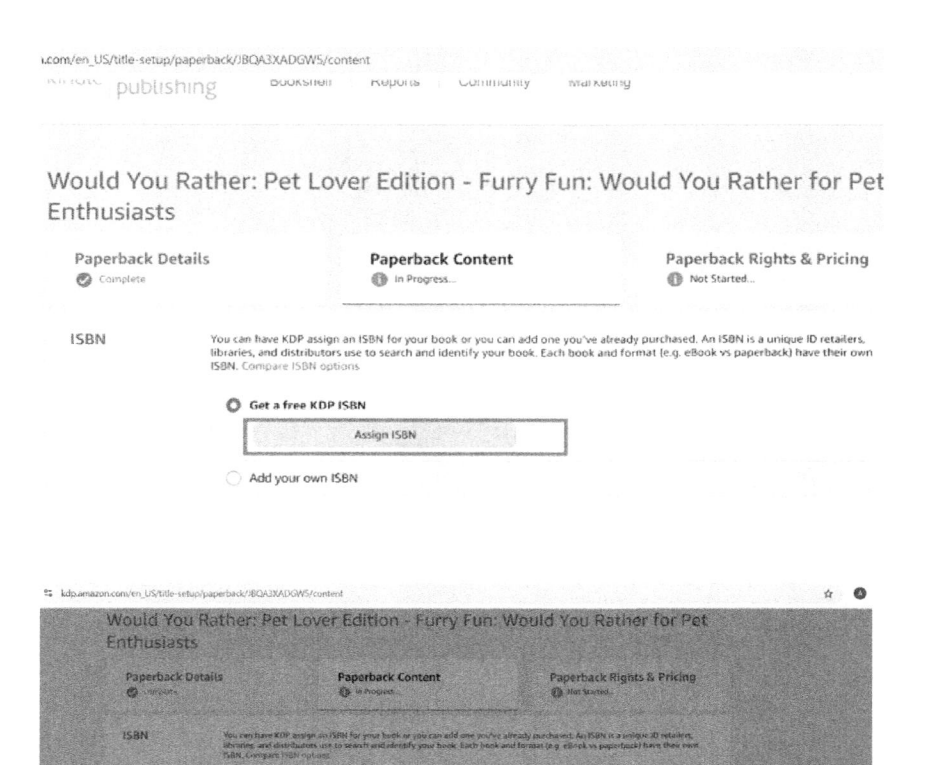

Step 13 : Print Options: we will choose according to the desired method, depending on the number of pages, the cost will increase from top to bottom

Trim size (book content size): choose according to your design.

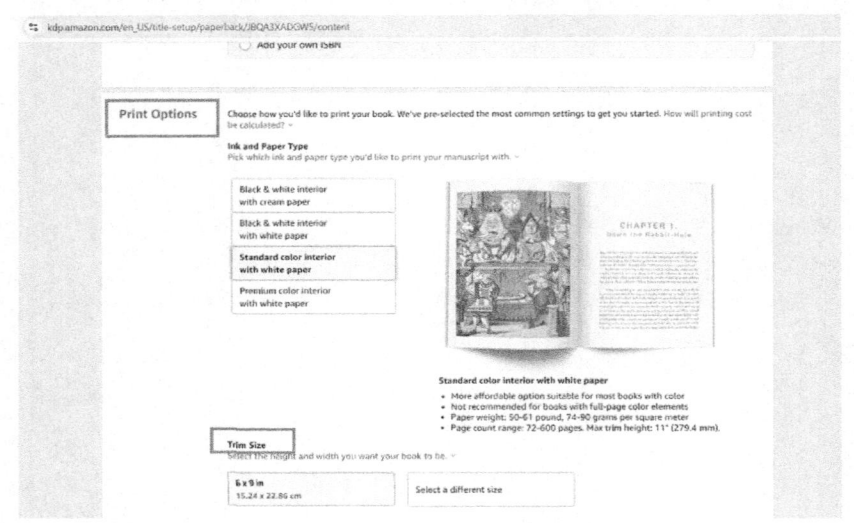

Bleed settings: choose bleed if the design is full screen, no bleed if the design is not full screen. Cover finish: choose matte to get the basic color, and dark cover design is suitable for glossy

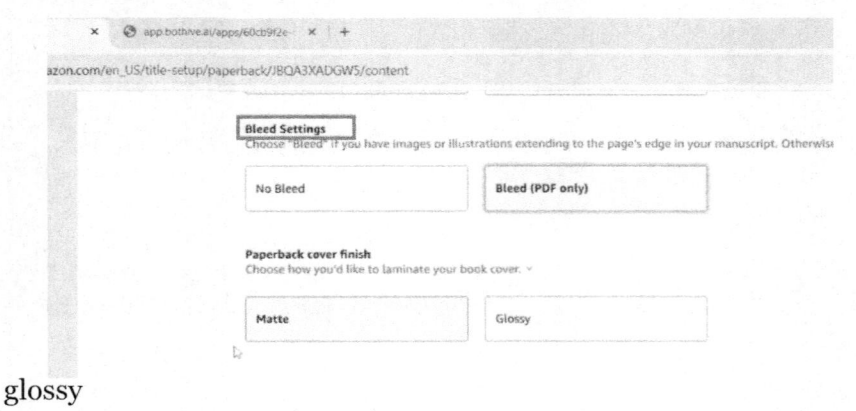

Step 14 : Manuscript section: for the book body, we choose upload to upload the PDF file created before. Book cover section: for the book cover, we choose upload your cover file to upload our cover design file.

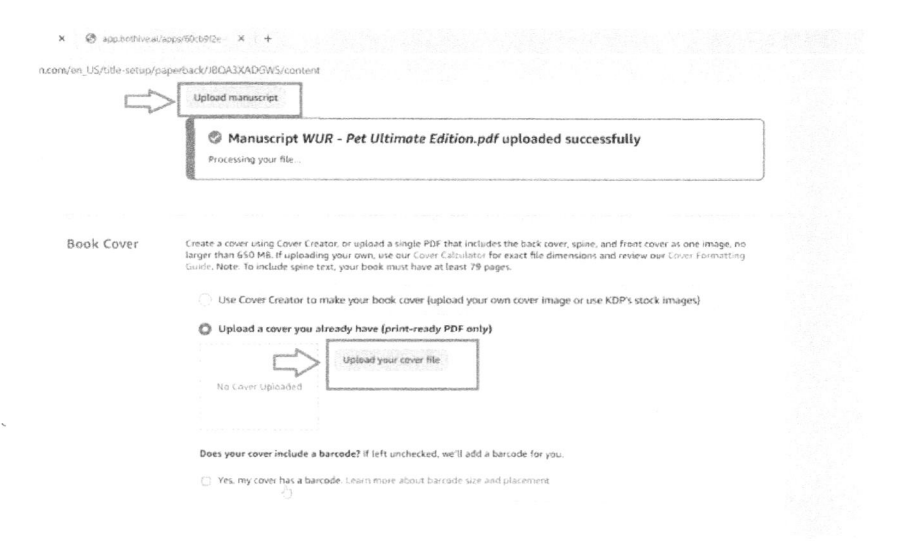

Step 15 : AI-Generated content section: we choose the AI parts to generate content.

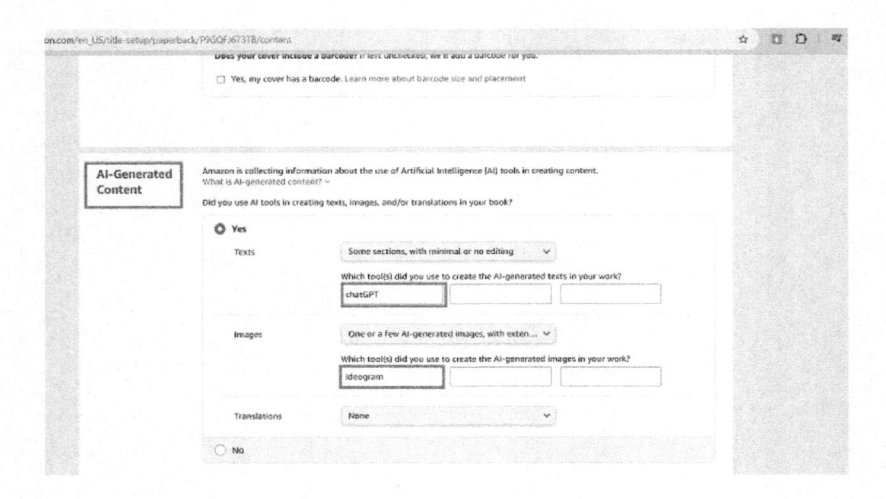

Step 16 : Once done, select Launch Previewer to preview the content before publishing.

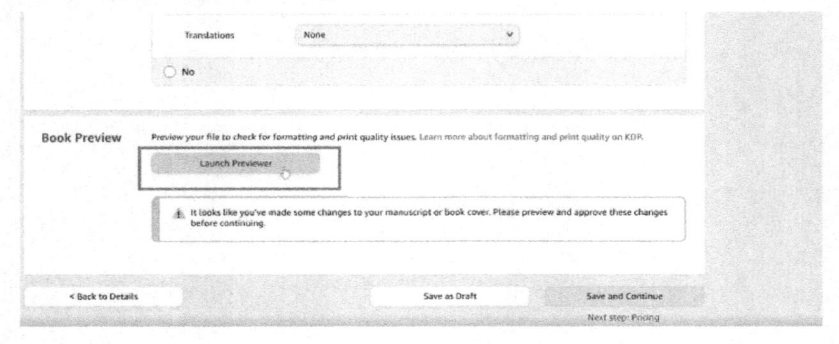

Preview mode #1:

Preview mode #2:

This is the interface to preview the content and quality before publishing. If there are no problems, select Approve to complete this step.

Step 17 : We choose save and continue to go to the next step.

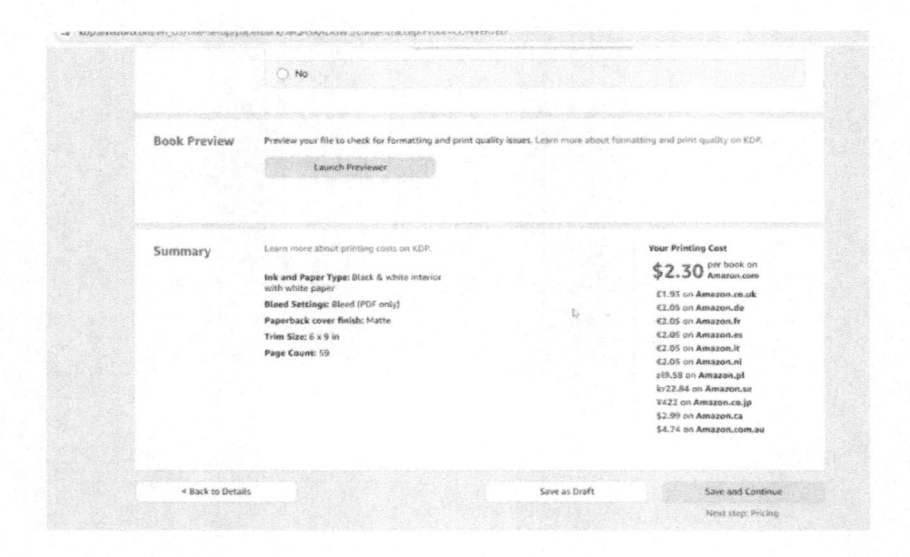

Step 18 : In the Territories interface, if there is no restriction on any territory, we choose the default.

In the pricing, royalties, and distribution section: we will fill in the price of the book, we will fill in the price that balances the market's acceptable selling price and the desired profit. After filling in the price for the main market amazon.com, the system will automatically convert the selling price for the remaining markets.

After publishing, the system needs 72 hours to process before the book is purchased by the customer. During this time, we can put the sample book back with the request proof feature.

So we have completed the steps to publish the book on Amazon, we choose publish your paperback book to complete the process.

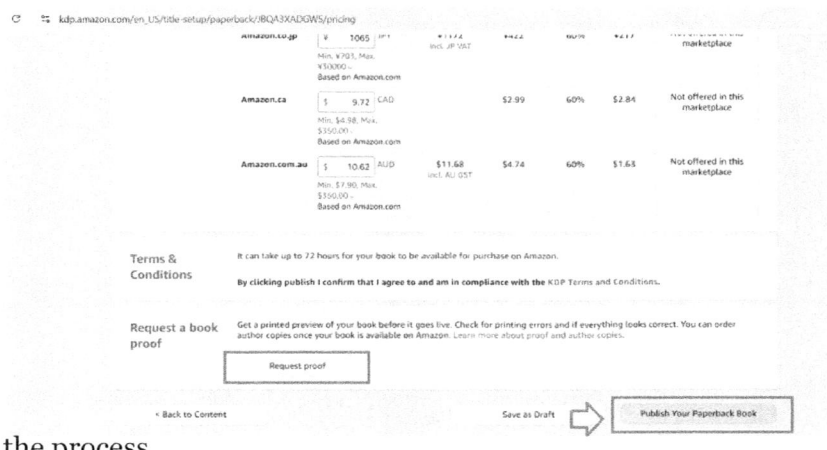

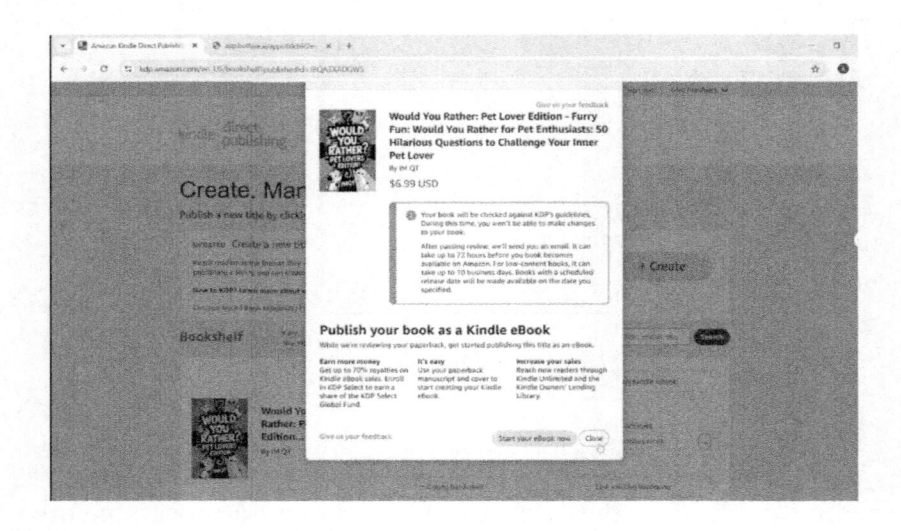

Back to the bookshelf section we will see our book here in "IN REVIEW" status.

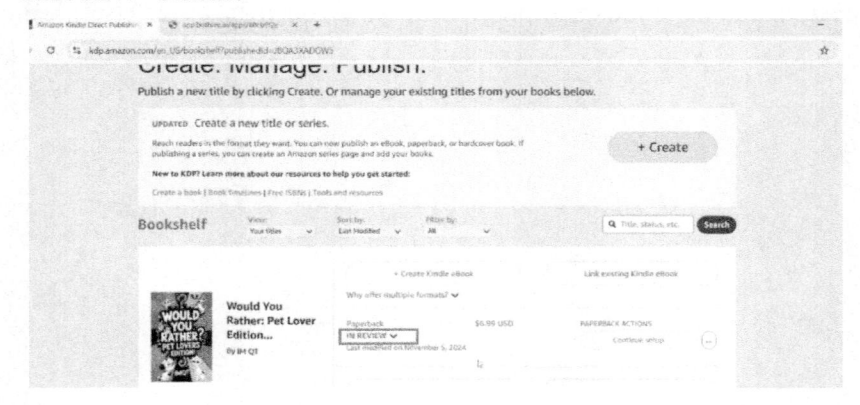

Once approved, your book will move to "LIVE" status.

Furry Festivities: Would You Rather...
By IM QT

Paperback
LIVE
Submitted on November 20, 2024

$13.99 USD
View on Amazon
ASIN: B0DNNJH9KT

+ Create hardcover

Why offer multiple formats?

SO WE HAVE SUCCESSFULLY PUBLISHED OUR BOOK ON AMAZON

WISH YOU SUCCESSFUL BOOK PUBLISHING !

Section 4: Strategic Pricing for Maximum Profits

Pricing as a Key Strategy

Setting the right price for your book is critical to its success. The price must appeal to your target audience, align with your competition, and still provide you with profitable returns. In this section, we'll delve into strategies for pricing eBooks, paperbacks, and hardcovers effectively on Amazon KDP, ensuring maximum sales and royalties.

1. Understanding Amazon KDP's Royalty Options

Amazon offers two royalty options for eBooks, each with specific pricing requirements:

1. The 35% Royalty Plan:

- Available for books priced below $2.99 or above $9.99.

- Best for niche or low-demand books where volume sales are unlikely.

2. The 70% Royalty Plan:

- Available for books priced between $2.99 and $9.99 in eligible countries.

- Ideal for popular or high-demand genres.

Pro Tip: Aim to price your eBook within the $2.99 to $9.99 range to qualify for the 70% royalty rate whenever possible.

2. Factors to Consider When Pricing

- **Audience Expectations:**

- Research the average price range for books in your niche.

- Example: Romance novels often sell for $3.99–$4.99, while detailed non-fiction books might range from $7.99–$9.99.

- Production Costs (for Print Books):

- Paperback and hardcover prices must account for printing costs.

- Amazon's pricing calculator can help you determine the minimum price required for profitability.

- Competition Analysis:

- Study competing titles in your niche to identify pricing trends.

- Avoid pricing too high above competitors unless your book offers significantly more value.

- Psychological Pricing:

- Use pricing strategies like $4.99 instead of $5.00 to make the price feel more appealing.

3. Pricing Strategies for Different Book Types

- eBooks:

- **Launch Pricing:** Start with a lower price ($0.99–$1.99) during the initial release to attract early buyers and build reviews.

- **Long-Term Pricing:** Gradually increase the price once the book gains traction and positive reviews.

- Paperbacks:

- **Cost-Based Pricing:** Factor in printing costs and desired royalties.

  ☐ Example: If the printing cost is $4.50 and you want a $3 royalty per sale, the minimum price should be $7.50.

- **Premium Pricing:** Position your book as a high-value item if it includes unique features like premium paper or extensive illustrations.

- Low-Content Books (e.g., Journals):

- Pricing typically ranges between $6.99 and $9.99, depending on the niche and design quality.

-Audiobooks:

- Use platforms like Audible to distribute your audiobook and set pricing in line with similar titles in your genre.

4. Using Amazon's Pricing Tools

Amazon provides several tools to help authors optimize their book pricing.

- KDP Pricing Calculator:

- Use this tool to calculate printing costs and potential royalties for print books.

- Comparative Pricing Insights:

- When setting your price, Amazon displays comparative pricing for similar books in your category.

-Promotional Pricing:

- Use **Kindle Countdown Deals** to offer time-limited discounts while retaining 70% royalties.

- Example: Offer your $4.99 book for $2.99 during launch week to boost visibility.

-Free Promotions:

- Set your eBook to $0 for up to 5 days per 90-day enrollment in KDP Select.
- Great for generating downloads, reviews, and exposure.

5. Testing and Adjusting Prices

Pricing is not static. Experimenting with different price points can help you find the sweet spot for maximizing sales and profits.

How to Test Pricing:

- Monitor Performance:

 Track sales, rankings, and reviews after changing your book's price.

- Run A/B Tests:

 Alternate pricing between two points (e.g., $2.99 and $3.99) and compare sales performance.

- Analyze Royalty Impact:

 Use Amazon's reporting tools to evaluate how pricing changes affect overall royalties.

6. Case Study: Pricing a Non-Fiction Self-Help Book

Scenario:
A non-fiction self-help book titled *"Breaking the Habit: A Guide to Building Discipline."*

Steps Taken:

- Research:

    ☐ Competitor prices ranged between $3.99 and $7.99.

- Launch Strategy:

    ☐ Set the eBook price at $0.99 during the first week to drive downloads and collect reviews.

- Long-Term Pricing:

    ☐ Gradually increased the price to $4.99, aligning with market trends.

- Promotions:

    ☐ Ran Kindle Countdown Deals twice during the first 90 days, pricing the book at $2.99 for a limited time.

Result: The book achieved 1,500 downloads during the launch week and consistently generated $500/month in royalties after reaching the $4.99 price point.

7. Common Pricing Mistakes to Avoid

- Pricing Too High Initially:

- Overpricing can deter early buyers and limit your book's visibility.

- Ignoring Printing Costs:

- For print books, ensure your price covers printing expenses while leaving room for profit.

-Underpricing High-Value Content:

- Avoid undervaluing books with extensive research, illustrations, or unique features.

- Failing to Test and Adjust Prices:

• Sticking to one price point without evaluating performance may limit your earnings.

Price Smart, Earn More

Strategic pricing is both an art and a science. By understanding your audience, leveraging Amazon's tools, and experimenting with price points, you can maximize sales and royalties for your books. Remember, the right price is one that reflects the value of your book while appealing to your target market.

Section 5: Pre-Publish Checklist and Launch Strategies

Setting the Stage for Success

Before hitting "Publish" on Amazon KDP, a thorough pre-publish checklist ensures your book is polished, professional, and ready to captivate readers. Beyond preparation, a solid launch strategy is essential for maximizing visibility, sales, and long-term success. This section provides a comprehensive guide to preparing your book for publication and executing a powerful launch.

Pre-Publish Checklist

1. Finalize Your Manuscript:

• **Proofread and Edit:**

- Use tools like Grammarly or ProWritingAid to check grammar, spelling, and readability.
- Hire a professional editor for an additional layer of polish.

- **Beta Readers:**
- Share your book with a small group of readers for feedback on content, flow, and clarity.

2. Verify Formatting:

- Ensure the manuscript is formatted correctly for both eBook and print editions.
- Check margins, spacing, and font consistency.
- Test your book in the KDP Previewer to verify its appearance on various devices.

3. Optimize Metadata:

- **Book Title and Subtitle:**
- Ensure these include relevant keywords for SEO.

- **Description:**
- Write a compelling synopsis highlighting your book's value to readers. Use bullet points for key features.

- **Categories and Keywords:**
- Choose two accurate categories on KDP.
- Use tools like Publisher Rocket to find high-performing keywords.

4. Design a Winning Cover:

- Ensure your cover aligns with genre expectations and grabs attention.

- Test different designs with potential readers or through social media polls.

5. Include a Call-to-Action (CTA):

- Add CTAs in your book for readers to leave reviews, follow your social media, or visit your website.

- Example: *"Loved this book? Leave a review on Amazon and share your thoughts!"*

Launch Strategies

1. Build Buzz Before the Launch:

- **Social Media Marketing:**
  - Post teasers, behind-the-scenes content, and countdowns on platforms like Instagram and TikTok.
  - Use hashtags relevant to your niche (e.g., #KindleReads, #NewRelease).

- **Email Marketing:**
  - Send a pre-launch email to your list, offering exclusive access or discounts.
  - Example: *"Be the first to grab my new book—available at a special launch price for the next 48 hours!"*

- **Collaborate with Influencers:**
  - Partner with bloggers, YouTubers, or Instagram influencers to promote your book.

2. Launch Week Pricing:

- Start with a discounted launch price to encourage early sales and reviews.

- Consider setting your eBook to $0.99 or running a **Kindle Countdown Deal**.

3. Leverage KDP Select:

- Enroll your book in KDP Select to benefit from:
  - Inclusion in Kindle Unlimited.
  - Access to Free Promotions and Kindle Countdown Deals.

4. Encourage Early Reviews:

- Reach out to beta readers and ARC (Advance Review Copy) reviewers to leave reviews on launch day.
- Make it easy by providing direct links to your book's Amazon page.

5. Run Amazon Ads:

- Start with Sponsored Product Ads targeting relevant keywords and categories.
- Set a modest daily budget (e.g., $10–$20) to test ad performance.

Marketing After the Launch

1. Maintain Momentum:

- Post-launch, continue sharing content on social media to sustain interest.
- Examples: Share reader reviews, fan photos, or excerpts from your book.

2. Update Keywords and Categories:

- Analyze your book's performance and refine keywords or categories as needed.

3. Engage with Your Audience:

- Respond to reviews and comments on Amazon or social media.
- Build a community of readers who look forward to your future releases.

4. Run Seasonal Promotions:

- Use holidays or events to re-promote your book.
- Example: A self-help book on productivity could be marketed during New Year's resolutions.

Real-Life Example: Launching a Romance Novel

Scenario: An author was launching a romance novel titled *"Love in the Time of Winter."*

Steps Taken:

- Pre-Publish Preparation:

- Polished the manuscript with professional editing and beta reader feedback.
- Designed a visually stunning cover featuring a wintery landscape.

- Pre-Launch Buzz:

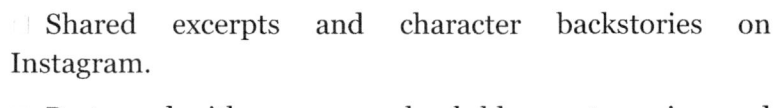

- Shared excerpts and character backstories on Instagram.
- Partnered with a romance book blogger to review and promote the book.

- Launch Week:

    ☐ Offered the eBook at $0.99 for the first week.

    ☐ Used KDP Select Free Promotions to generate over 1,000 downloads.

- Post-Launch:

    ☐ Ran Amazon Ads targeting keywords like "holiday romance" and "snowy love story."

    ☐ Garnered 50+ reviews within the first month, boosting the book's visibility in its category.

Result: The book became a bestseller in the "Holiday Romance" category, earning $1,200 in its first month.

Common Launch Mistakes to Avoid

1. Rushing the Launch:

- Take the time to proofread, test formatting, and optimize metadata before publishing.

2. Ignoring Pre-Launch Marketing:

- A strong pre-launch strategy creates anticipation and ensures immediate sales.

3. Underestimating the Power of Reviews:

- Reviews significantly impact your book's ranking and visibility.

4. Failing to Test Ads:

- Launching ads without testing different keywords or targeting options can waste your budget.

A Strong Start Leads to Long-Term Success

A successful book launch is the culmination of careful preparation and strategic marketing. By following this pre-publish checklist and implementing effective launch strategies, you can maximize your book's potential, boost initial sales, and set the foundation for long-term success on Amazon KDP.

Chapter 4: Marketing and Traffic Strategies

Objective: Teach readers how to drive traffic, maximize book sales, and establish a lasting presence on Amazon by leveraging SEO, marketing tools, and strategic promotion.

Section 1: Mastering Amazon's Built-In Marketing Tools

Amazon's marketing tools are designed to help authors like you connect with readers, drive visibility, and boost sales. The key is understanding how to use these tools effectively and optimize them to align with your book's goals.

Amazon SEO: How It Works and How to Use It for Success

Amazon's search engine algorithm, known as **A9**, plays a critical role in determining how your book ranks in search results. By understanding how Amazon SEO works and applying best practices, you can significantly boost your book's visibility, attract readers, and maximize sales.

1. Understanding How Amazon SEO Works

Amazon's A9 algorithm evaluates multiple factors to rank products (including books) in search results. Here's how it operates:

Key Factors Affecting Amazon SEO

- Keywords:

- Keywords in your book's title, subtitle, backend metadata, and description are crucial.

- Amazon uses these keywords to match your book with search queries.

- Sales Performance:

- Books with consistent sales rank higher in search results.

- The more frequently your book is purchased, the stronger its visibility.

- Conversion Rate:

- High conversion rates (e.g., readers clicking and buying after viewing your book) indicate relevance and quality to Amazon.

- Customer Reviews:

- Positive reviews improve your book's ranking by signaling trustworthiness.

- Categories and Subcategories:

- Placing your book in appropriate and niche categories makes it easier for readers to find it.

2. Implementing Amazon SEO to Rank Keywords

Amazon SEO starts with selecting the right keywords and strategically placing them throughout your book's metadata.

Step 1: Conducting Keyword Research

Tools for Keyword Research:

Publisher Rocket:

- Provides search volumes, competition levels, and estimated earnings for keywords.

☐ Example: If you search for "self-help journal," Publisher Rocket might suggest related keywords like "mindfulness journal" or "daily gratitude journal."

Google Trends:

☐ Track the popularity of keywords over time to identify trends.

Amazon Search Bar Autocomplete:

☐ Type a keyword into Amazon's search bar and note the autocomplete suggestions.

Criteria for Choosing Keywords:

- High search volume.
- Low to medium competition.
- Relevant to your book's theme.

Step 2: Optimizing Metadata

Where to Place Keywords:

Title and Subtitle:

☐ Include primary keywords naturally.

- Example: *"Mindful Moments: A Guided Journal for Beginners"* combines "mindfulness" and "journal."

Backend Keywords (Metadata):

☐ Use all 7 backend keyword slots provided by Amazon.

☐ Avoid repeating keywords already in your title or subtitle.

☐ Include variations, synonyms, and related terms.

Book Description:

⬜ Write a compelling description that naturally incorporates keywords.

⬜ Use HTML formatting (e.g., bold or italic text) for readability.

- Example: *"This mindfulness journal is perfect for beginners seeking to reduce stress and find inner peace."*

Categories and Subcategories:

⬜ Choose categories that align with your book's content.

⬜ Use tools like Publisher Rocket to identify niche subcategories where competition is lower.

- Example: Instead of "Self-Help," choose "Self-Help > Journaling."

Step 3: Boosting Initial Sales for SEO

Initial sales play a major role in ranking your book for targeted keywords.

Strategies to Drive Early Sales:

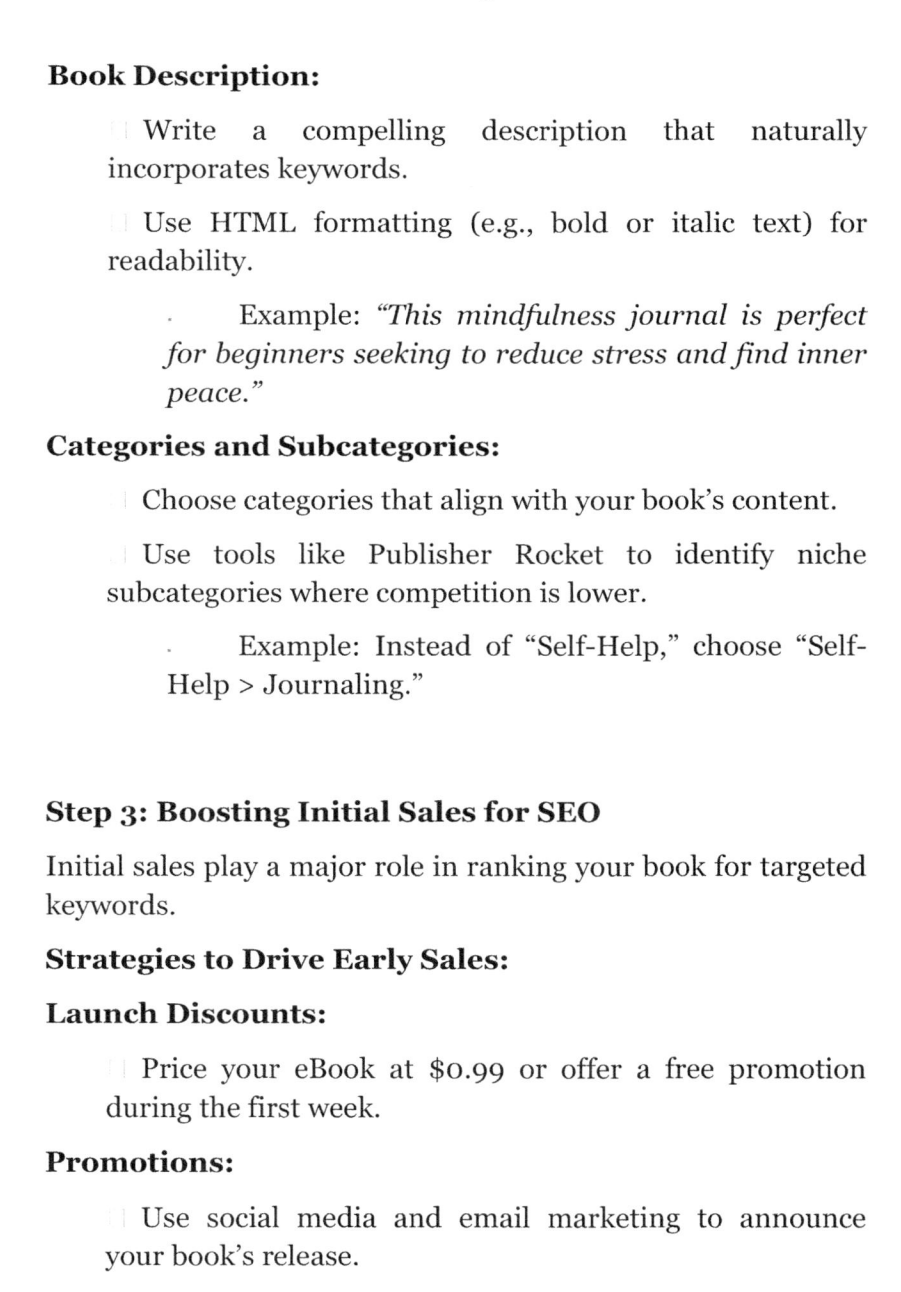

Launch Discounts:

⬜ Price your eBook at $0.99 or offer a free promotion during the first week.

Promotions:

⬜ Use social media and email marketing to announce your book's release.

Amazon Ads:

☐ Run Sponsored Product ads targeting your primary keywords.

Step 4: Encouraging Reviews

How Reviews Impact SEO:

- Reviews boost credibility and signal to Amazon that your book is relevant.
- Books with more reviews rank higher for their target keywords.

How to Get Reviews:

Reach out to beta readers or ARC reviewers.

Include a request for reviews at the end of your book:

☐ Example: *"If you enjoyed this book, consider leaving a review to help others discover it!"*

3. Tracking SEO Performance

To ensure your efforts are working, monitor your book's ranking and adjust your strategies as needed.

Tools for Monitoring Performance:

Amazon Author Dashboard:

☐ Track your book's sales rank and page reads.

BookBeam:

☐ Provides insights into keyword performance and category rankings.

Publisher Rocket:

- Revisit keyword data to refine your metadata based on performance.

4. Real-Life Example: Ranking a Coloring Book

Scenario: An author published a coloring book for adults focused on stress relief.

Steps Taken:

Keyword Research:

- Identified keywords like "stress relief coloring book" and "mandala designs for relaxation" using Publisher Rocket.

Metadata Optimization:

- Title: *"Stress Relief Mandalas: A Coloring Book for Relaxation and Mindfulness."*

- Backend Keywords: Included "stress relief," "adult coloring," "mindfulness mandalas," and "relaxation activities."

Launch Strategy:

- Offered the eBook at $0.99 for the first week.

- Ran Sponsored Product ads targeting primary keywords.

Review Strategy:

- Sent free copies to reviewers and asked them to leave honest feedback.

Result:
The book ranked in the top 5 for "stress relief coloring book" within 30 days, generating consistent daily sales.

5. Common SEO Mistakes to Avoid

Overloading Metadata:

  ☐ Avoid keyword stuffing; it can make your metadata look spammy.

Choosing Generic Keywords:

  ☐ Keywords like "journal" or "novel" are too broad and competitive.

Ignoring Backend Keywords:

  ☐ Failing to use all available keyword slots reduces your book's search potential.

Neglecting Reviews:

  ☐ Fewer reviews can hurt your ranking, even with good SEO.

Conclusion: Master Amazon SEO for Success

Amazon SEO is the foundation of a successful book marketing strategy. By understanding how A9 works, choosing the right keywords, and optimizing your metadata, you can position your book for long-term visibility and sales. Combine these tactics with promotional efforts and analytics to refine your approach and ensure ongoing success.

Amazon Ads: How to Use Them to Drive Book Sales

Amazon Ads is one of the most effective tools for promoting your book on the platform. It allows you to target specific audiences, increase your book's visibility, and drive consistent sales. However, to make the most of Amazon Ads, you need to understand the types of ads available, how to set them up, and how to optimize them for maximum ROI.

1. Types of Amazon Ads

- Sponsored Products

- **What It Does:** Promotes individual books by displaying them in search results and product pages.

- **Best For:** Authors looking to increase visibility for a single title.

- **Example Placement:**
  - Search result for "self-help books."
  - "Sponsored" label on a product page.

- Sponsored Brands

- **What It Does:** Highlights your author brand or multiple books in a banner ad at the top of search results.

- **Best For:** Authors with a series or multiple titles in the same genre.

- **Features:** Custom headline and logo to build brand recognition.

- Sponsored Display

- **What It Does:** Retargets readers who've browsed similar books or genres.

- **Best For:** Reaching potential buyers who are already interested in your niche.
- **Placement:** Ads appear on Amazon-owned properties and devices, such as Kindle and Fire tablets.

2. Setting Up an Amazon Ad Campaign

When setting up your advertising campaign for the first time, Amazon will prompt you to establish your payment profile in two simple steps:

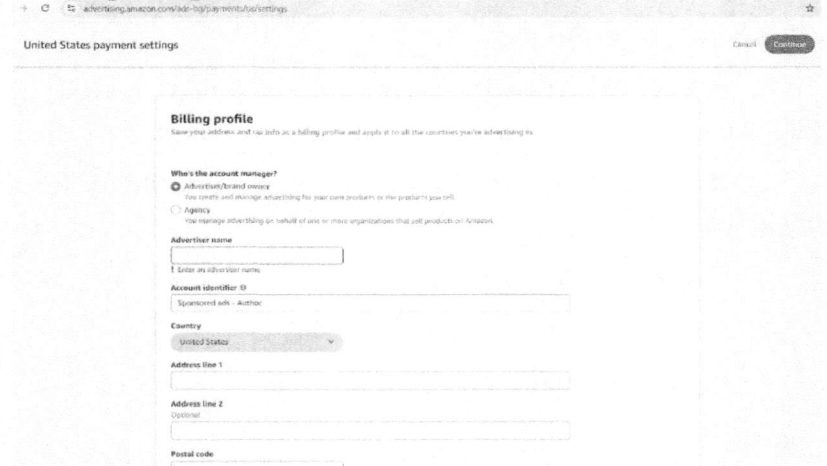

The Billing Profile and Payment Profile sections require you to enter your information along with any accepted payment methods, such as Visa, MasterCard, or other major credit and debit cards.

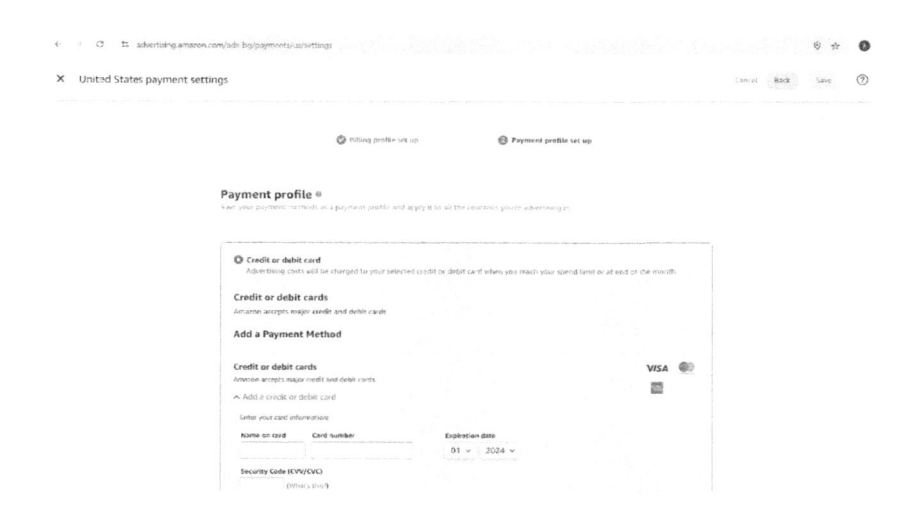

Step 1: Define Your Campaign Goal

•   **Visibility:** Target broader keywords to maximize impressions.

•   **Sales:** Focus on high-intent keywords (e.g., "buy mindfulness coloring book").

Step 2: Research Keywords

Effective keyword targeting is essential for Amazon Ads.

Tools to Use:

Publisher Rocket: Provides insights into high-traffic, low-competition keywords.

Amazon Search Bar: Use autocomplete suggestions to find relevant phrases.

Types of Keywords to Target:

- **Exact Match:** Targets searches identical to your keyword.
- **Phrase Match:** Targets searches that include your keyword phrase.
- **Broad Match:** Targets searches related to your keyword.

Example for a Children's Book:
- Exact Match: "bedtime stories for toddlers."
- Phrase Match: "stories for toddlers."
- Broad Match: "books for toddlers."

Step 3: Create the Campaign

1. Log into your Amazon KDP dashboard and access the **Amazon Advertising Console.**

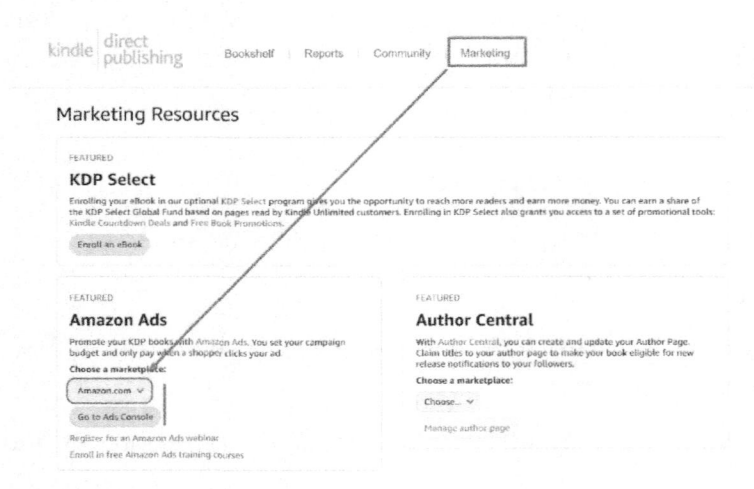

Then click "Create Campaign" to create your first campaign.

2. Choose a campaign type: Sponsored Products is ideal for most authors.

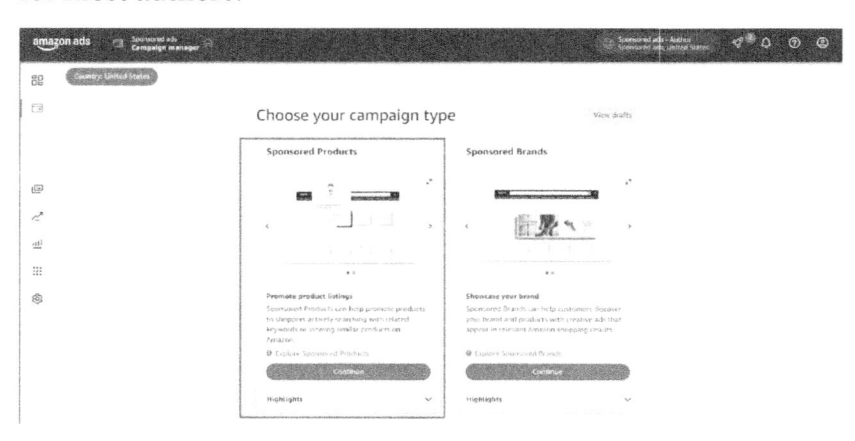

There will be several requirements per campaign:

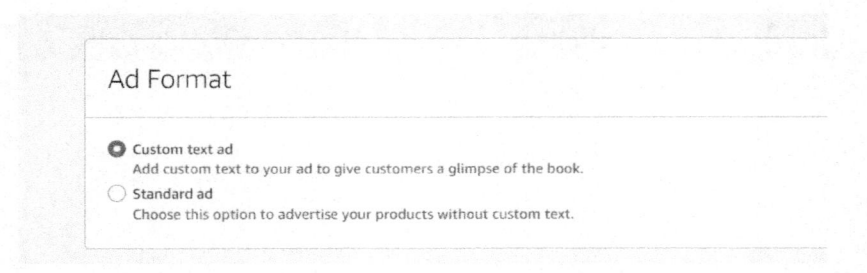

- Ad Format:
    - Custom text ad: Amazon will permit us to display text ads in which we can write custom text to draw readers to our books. Custom text displays on product detail pages.
    - Standard ad: The book will be advertised with its title and image only.
- Next component of the campaign, "Products": Add books that you want to promote into the campaign. These are the books in your KDP bookshelf or that you've claimed in your Author Central account.

Here you can add as little as one book per campaign or as much as 1000 titles. But you should only add one book for one campaign or the titles with the same advertising purpose.

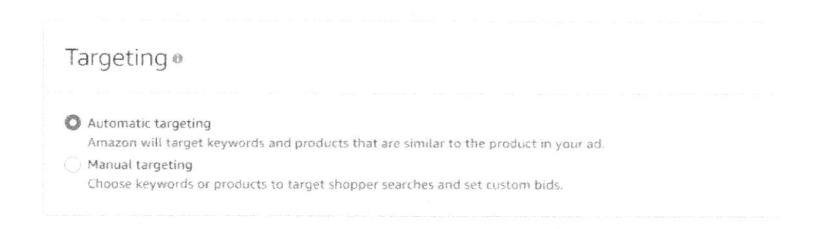

- The next important component of a campaign is "Targeting, there will be 2 options here:
  - Automatic targeting: Amazon will utilize its algorithm to suggest your books for the most relevant keywords and products.
  - Manual targeting: This option gives you some control over selecting the keywords or products you wish to target.

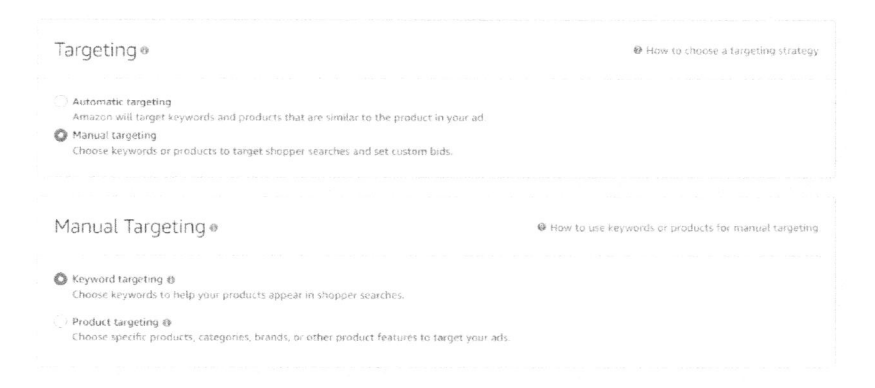

Let's discover the Manual Targeting option first:

Quick Tip: Amazon always provides an ⓘ icon for further explanation.

With Keyword targeting, Amazon allows us to either use their "suggested" keywords or we can manually add our *researched keywords* under the "Enter list" tab or bulk upload them with the "Upload file".

There are several things to remember here:

- The 'Bid' option: Suggested bid (by Amazon) / Custom bid & Default bid (by Author)
- The 'Filter by' options include Broad, Phrase, and Exact. Each option works with different principles
- 'Sort by' option: Orders/Clicks. After you insert your book, the keywords will appear on the "Keyword" table

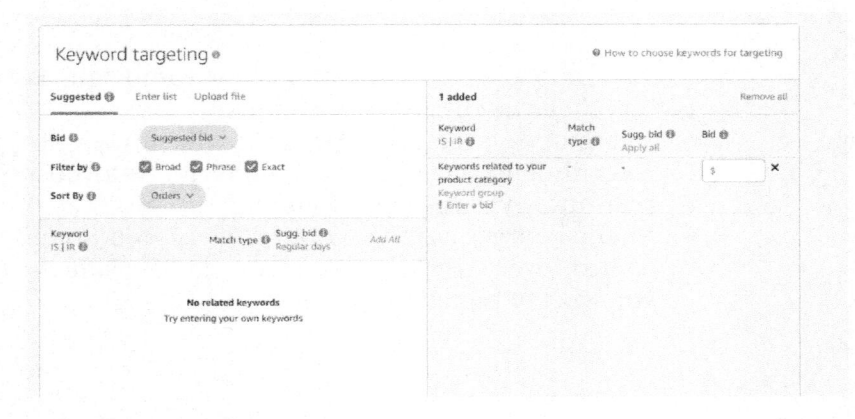

Under the Keyword targeting tab, it's the Negative keyword targeting tab:

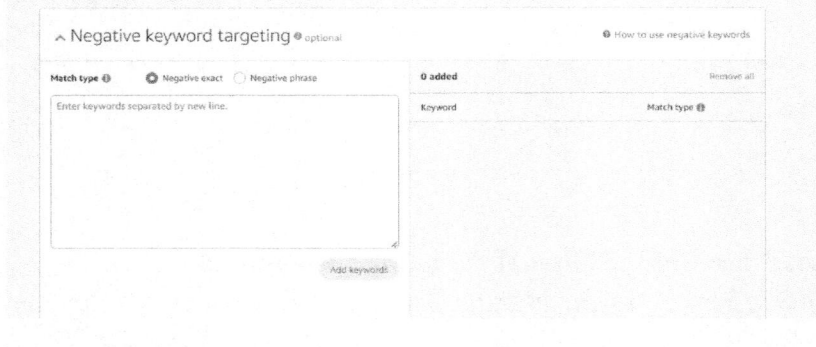

In line with its name, you can negate irrelevant keywords by adding them one by one to the table.

And here is the 'Negative product targeting' tab if you choose to target products in the previous step

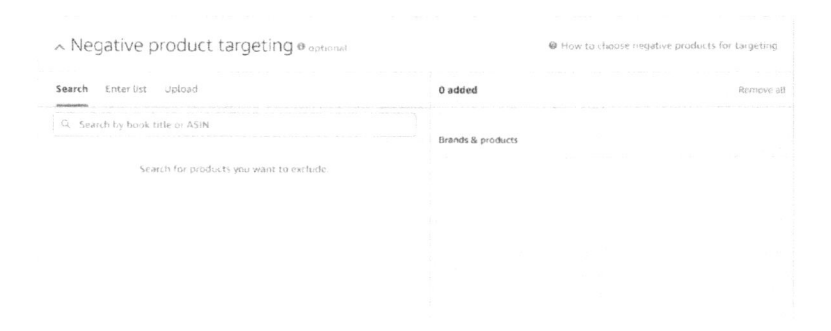

- The next element of the campaign is the 'bidding strategy,' which allows us to determine how we will place bids for our keywords on Amazon.

These settings will influence our bidding throughout the campaign. With the 'up and down' option, Amazon can increase the bid by up to 100% of the current amount. While this setting can generate more impressions for our books, it may quickly deplete the total budget. Based on my experience, it's advisable to choose 'down only' along with the subsequent 'bid adjustments':

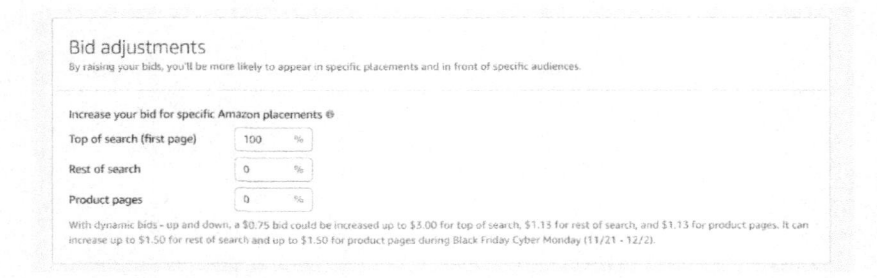

Lastly, the 'Settings' tab for our campaign:

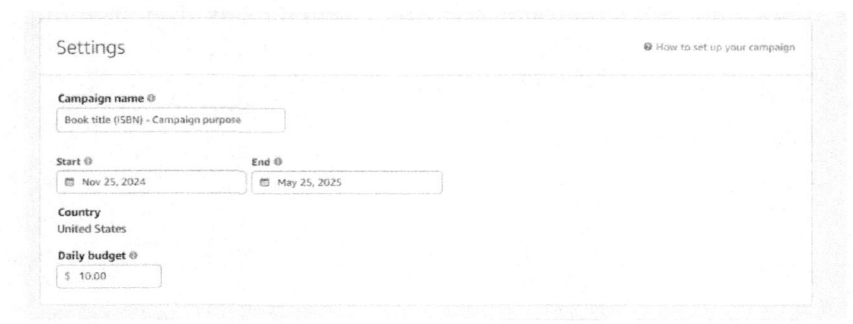

When naming the campaign, it's advisable to include the title of our book along with the campaign's objective. For instance, we could start with 'Book 1 - Discovery' and later transition to 'Book 1 - Profit Optimization'. The start date should match the date we set for our campaign or be a future date. The end date can either remain at the default setting of 'no end date' or be specified. The daily budget varies for each author, but starting with $10 per day is a solid choice.

In Automatic Targeting campaigns, there is a notable distinction: rather than manually inputting keywords, Amazon allows us to establish a single bid for four groups or to set bids individually for each group

- Close match: show ads to shoppers who use search terms closely related to our books.
- Loose match: show ads to shoppers who use search terms loosely related to our books.
- Substitutes: show ads to shoppers who use detail pages of products similar to our books
- Complements: to shoppers who view the detail pages of products that complement our books (If the title is 'Mystery at Midnight,' Amazon will display an ad on detail pages that feature related items such as 'Best Mystery Novels' and 'Thrilling Page-Turners.')

These other settings are the same as those for manual campaigns.

Step 4: Write Engaging Ad Copy

If applicable (e.g., for Sponsored Brands), create a compelling headline.

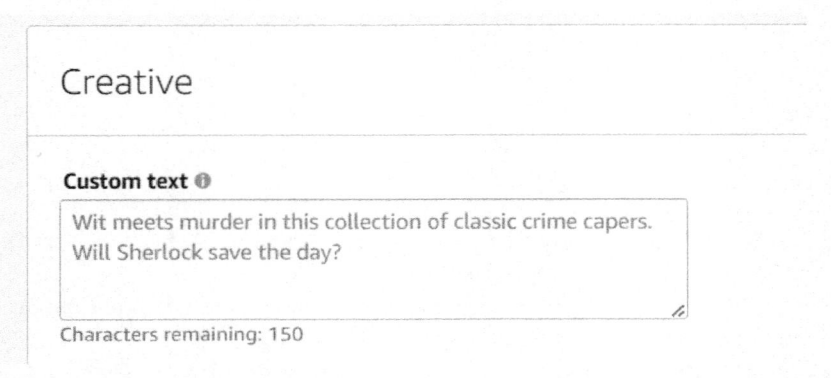

• Example: "Transform Your Life with the Ultimate Mindfulness Journal."

3. Optimizing Amazon Ads for Success

- Monitor Performance Metrics

Track these key metrics in your Amazon Ads dashboard:

• **CTR (Click-Through Rate):** The percentage of people who click your ad after seeing it. Aim for at least 0.5%.

• **CPC (Cost Per Click):** The amount you pay per click. Lower CPC indicates better efficiency.

• **ACOS (Advertising Cost of Sales):** The percentage of sales spent on ads. Aim for an ACOS below 50%.

- Use Xmars AI for Automation

Xmars AI simplifies ad management by:

• Automatically adjusting bids for underperforming keywords.

- Identifying top-performing keywords and allocating more budget to them.

- A/B Test Campaigns

Test variations of:

- Keywords: Compare broad match vs. exact match.
- Bids: Start low and gradually increase for competitive keywords.
- Ad Copy: Experiment with different headlines or descriptions.

- Refine Targeting

- Pause ads targeting keywords with high impressions but low CTR.
- Focus on keywords generating consistent clicks and conversions.

4. Maximizing ROI with Amazon Ads

- Start with Automatic Targeting

- Allows Amazon to match your book with relevant search terms and categories.
- Analyze results to identify high-performing keywords.

- Gradually Transition to Manual Targeting

- Focus on specific keywords and categories that performed well in automatic campaigns.

- Scale Winning Campaigns

- Increase daily budgets and bids for campaigns with high ROI.

- Expand to Sponsored Brands or Display Ads once Sponsored Products campaigns are optimized.

5. Real-Life Example: Advertising a Self-Help eBook

Scenario:

An author launched a self-help eBook titled *"Breaking Free: Overcoming Anxiety Through Mindfulness."*

Steps Taken:

- Keyword Research:

    Used Publisher Rocket to target phrases like "anxiety mindfulness techniques" and "mindfulness for beginners."

- Campaign Setup:

    Created a Sponsored Product campaign with a $15 daily budget.

    Ran a separate automatic targeting campaign to discover additional keywords.

- Optimization:

    Paused underperforming keywords with low CTR.

    Increased bids on keywords generating sales, such as "overcoming anxiety book."

- Result:

    Achieved a 10% ACOS with a CTR of 1.5%.

    Generated $1,200 in additional royalties within the first month.

6. Common Mistakes to Avoid

- Underbidding for Competitive Keywords:

•	Competitive keywords may require higher bids to gain visibility.

- Ignoring Negative Keywords:

•	Use negative keywords to exclude irrelevant searches and improve targeting.

　　Example: Exclude "free" to avoid clicks from users searching for free books.

- Setting and Forgetting Campaigns:

•	Regularly review performance and adjust bids or keywords to maintain effectiveness.

Master Amazon Ads for Long-Term Growth

Amazon Ads is a powerful tool for driving visibility and sales, but success requires strategic planning, continuous optimization, and data-driven decisions. By researching keywords, monitoring performance, and refining your approach, you can build campaigns that deliver consistent returns and help your book climb the rankings.

Xmars AI: The Ultimate Tool for Amazon Ad Optimization

Xmars AI is a cutting-edge platform specifically designed to enhance the efficiency of Amazon ad campaigns. By leveraging artificial intelligence, it simplifies the complexities of ad management, enabling authors to maximize visibility and sales while optimizing ad spend.

1. What is Xmars AI?

Xmars AI is an all-in-one Amazon advertising tool that automates key aspects of campaign creation, optimization, and performance tracking. It's tailored to meet the needs of authors and sellers on Amazon, allowing them to focus on creating and selling while the platform handles the technicalities of ad performance.

Key Benefits of Xmars AI:

- Automated keyword and bid management.
- Advanced performance insights and analytics.
- Time-saving automation features for campaign adjustments.
- User-friendly dashboard for managing multiple campaigns.

2. Setting Up Xmars AI

Setting up Xmars AI is straightforward and requires linking your Amazon Ads account to the platform.

Step 1: Account Integration

1. Create an account on the Xmars AI platform.
2. Link your Amazon Advertising Console to Xmars AI.
   - This allows Xmars to access your campaign data for optimization.

Step 2: Configure Campaign Goals

- Define your objectives, such as:
  - Increasing sales for a specific book.
  - Reducing ACOS (Advertising Cost of Sales) to below 30%.
  - Boosting CTR (Click-Through Rate) to above 0.8%.
- Set a daily or monthly budget for your campaigns.

Step 3: Upload Campaign Data

- If you already have running campaigns, Xmars will import them for analysis and optimization.
- For new campaigns, you can set up directly on Xmars by entering your book details, keywords, and desired bids.

3. Features of Xmars AI

- Automated Bid Adjustments

Xmars AI dynamically adjusts your keyword bids based on performance metrics like CTR, CPC (Cost Per Click), and conversions.

- Ensures competitive bidding for high-performing keywords.

- Reduces spend on keywords with low ROI.

Example: If "mindfulness coloring book" performs well, Xmars increases the bid to keep your ad competitive. For poorly converting keywords, like "free mindfulness book," Xmars lowers or eliminates the bid.

- Keyword Research and Recommendations

- Xmars analyzes your campaign data and suggests high-performing keywords you might not have considered.
- Uses real-time trends to identify new opportunities.

How It Works:

- Xmars tracks buyer behavior and keyword trends across Amazon.
- It identifies "hidden gems" with high search volume and low competition.

- Performance Analytics Dashboard

Xmars provides an intuitive dashboard to monitor:

- CTR: Measures how effective your ad is at attracting clicks.
- CPC: Helps you control ad spend by showing the cost of each click.
- ACOS: The percentage of ad spend relative to sales. Lower ACOS means higher profitability.

- Negative Keyword Management

Prevent wasting ad spend by excluding irrelevant keywords.

- Example: If you're selling a paid eBook, Xmars can automatically exclude keywords like "free book."

- Campaign Automation

Automate repetitive tasks, such as:

- Adjusting bids based on performance.
- Testing new keywords to expand reach.
- Pausing low-performing campaigns.

- How to Use Xmars AI to Optimize Campaigns

Step 1: Identify Campaign Weaknesses

- Log into the Xmars dashboard and review the performance of your current campaigns.
- Look for high CPC or low CTR keywords that are inflating costs without driving sales.

Step 2: Implement Automated Bid Strategies

- Enable Xmars' automated bidding to optimize your ad spend:
  - Increase bids on keywords with high CTR and conversion rates.
  - Decrease or pause bids on low-performing keywords.

Step 3: Expand Keyword Targeting

- Use Xmars' keyword suggestions to identify additional terms related to your niche.
- Expand campaigns by targeting:
  - **Exact Match:** Highly specific terms like "mindfulness adult coloring book."
  - **Phrase Match:** Broader terms like "adult coloring book."

☐ **Broad Match:** General terms like "coloring book."

Step 4: Monitor and Refine

- Regularly review Xmars' performance reports to understand campaign ROI.

- Adjust campaign budgets based on the analytics provided.

Step 5: A/B Testing with Xmars

- Test multiple ad copies, keywords, or targeting options to determine the most effective combination.

- Example: Compare CTR and ACOS for two Sponsored Product campaigns with different sets of keywords.

- Real-Life Example: Optimizing Ads with Xmars AI

Scenario: An author launched a self-help eBook titled *"Stress-Free Living: A Mindfulness Guide."*

Steps Taken Using Xmars AI:

- Setup and Integration:

☐ Linked Amazon Ads account to Xmars AI.

☐ Imported existing ad campaigns for analysis.

- Campaign Optimization:

☐ Increased bids for high-performing keywords like "mindfulness for stress relief."

☐ Paused underperforming keywords such as "free stress book."

- Keyword Expansion:

◻ Added new keywords suggested by Xmars, including "mindfulness daily guide" and "stress-free techniques."

- Performance Tracking:

◻ Monitored CTR and adjusted bids daily for competitive terms.

◻ Reduced ACOS from 40% to 18% within two weeks.

Result:

• 30% increase in sales within the first month.

• $900 in monthly royalties directly attributed to optimized ad campaigns.

6. Common Mistakes to Avoid

Ignoring Negative Keywords:

◻ Failing to exclude irrelevant terms can inflate your ad spend.

Underutilizing Data:

◻ Xmars provides extensive analytics—use them to make informed decisions.

Setting and Forgetting Campaigns:

◻ Regularly review performance and make adjustments.

How AI Works in Xmars: Behind the Optimization

Xmars AI uses advanced algorithms and machine learning to analyze, manage, and optimize Amazon ad campaigns with precision and efficiency. Unlike manual management, Xmars continuously processes real-time data to identify trends, adjust strategies, and enhance ad performance without requiring constant user intervention. Here's a breakdown of how the AI behind Xmars operates and improves your campaigns.

1. Intelligent Bid Adjustments

One of the most impactful AI-driven features of Xmars is its ability to adjust keyword bids dynamically.

How It Works:

- Data Analysis:

   ☐ Xmars monitors your campaign data, including impressions, clicks, CTR, CPC, and conversion rates.

   ☐ It identifies which keywords are driving sales and which are consuming budget without converting.

- Automated Decision-Making:

   ☐ High-performing keywords: Increases bids to boost visibility and capture more impressions.

   ☐ Low-performing keywords: Decreases bids or pauses them entirely to minimize waste.

Example:
If "mindfulness journal for stress relief" has a high CTR and generates sales, Xmars increases its bid to ensure it outperforms competing ads. Meanwhile, if "self-help free guide" generates clicks but no sales, the AI reduces its bid or excludes the keyword altogether.

2. Predictive Analytics

Xmars AI predicts future trends based on historical data and market patterns.

How It Works:

- Pattern Recognition:

   Analyzes data from your campaigns and similar campaigns within the same category.

   Identifies patterns, such as seasonal spikes or time-of-day trends.

- Forecasting Performance:

   Predicts which keywords are likely to perform well based on trends, enabling proactive adjustments.

Example:
Before a holiday season, Xmars might notice increased searches for "gratitude journals" and recommend higher bids or additional keywords to capitalize on the trend.

3. Keyword Discovery and Expansion

Xmars AI continuously searches for new keyword opportunities to expand your ad reach.

How It Works:

- Semantic Analysis:

   Scans Amazon's search queries to identify keywords related to your book.

   Groups similar terms and synonyms to suggest variations for targeting.

- Search Volume and Competition Analysis:

   Ranks keywords by search volume and competition level, prioritizing those with high traffic and low competition.

Example:
If your primary keyword is "adult coloring book," Xmars might suggest related terms like "stress relief coloring book," "mindfulness mandalas," or "relaxation activities."

4. Negative Keyword Management

AI helps identify and exclude irrelevant keywords, ensuring ad spend is focused only on terms likely to convert.

How It Works:

- Behavioral Analysis:

  ☐ Tracks the performance of keywords generating clicks but no sales.

  ☐ Flags those with high costs and low conversions as candidates for exclusion.

- Automated Exclusions:

  ☐ Adds these underperforming terms to your campaign's negative keyword list.

Example:
For a paid eBook campaign, Xmars might automatically exclude terms like "free book" or "PDF download."

5. Real-Time Performance Monitoring

Xmars AI monitors campaign performance 24/7 and makes real-time adjustments to maximize ROI.

How It Works:

- Continuous Data Stream:

Processes new data as it becomes available, ensuring campaigns are always optimized for current conditions.

- Immediate Action:

Detects spikes in CTR or CPC and adjusts bids or budgets instantly to capitalize on opportunities or reduce waste.

Example: If a keyword suddenly gains traction during a peak search period, Xmars boosts its bid to maintain visibility while the demand lasts.

6. Campaign Segmentation and Personalization

Xmars uses AI to segment campaigns based on performance metrics and audience behavior.

How It Works:

- Segmentation:

Separates keywords into categories based on performance (e.g., high, medium, or low-converting terms).

- Personalized Strategies:

Applies tailored bid strategies for each segment:

- High-converting keywords: Increase bids and budgets.

- Low-converting keywords: Test alternative match types or pause.

Example:
If "journaling prompts for anxiety" performs well, Xmars shifts more budget toward it while pausing a similar underperforming keyword like "journal for stress relief."

7. Advanced Reporting and Insights

Xmars AI doesn't just optimize campaigns; it provides actionable insights to help you understand what's working.

How It Works:

- Data Visualization:

  ☐ Presents campaign performance metrics in easy-to-read graphs and dashboards.

- Actionable Insights:

  ☐ Highlights opportunities to expand successful campaigns or improve weaker ones.

- Custom Reports:

  ☐ Generates reports tailored to your goals, such as ACOS reduction or sales growth.

Example: You might receive a report showing that Sponsored Display ads targeting "mindfulness for beginners" have a higher ROI than Sponsored Product ads, prompting you to reallocate your budget.

8. Machine Learning for Continuous Improvement

Xmars AI becomes smarter over time by learning from your campaigns.

How It Works:

- Feedback Loop:

  ☐ Every adjustment and its outcome are analyzed to refine future strategies.

- Self-Optimization:

    Learns which keywords, bids, and strategies are most effective for your specific book and niche.

Example:
After running multiple campaigns for a children's storybook, Xmars learns that terms like "bedtime stories" convert better on weekends and automatically increases bids during those times.

9. How to Maximize the Benefits of Xmars AI

Set Clear Goals:

    Define objectives like increasing sales, reducing ACOS, or improving CTR.

Regularly Review Insights:

    Use the reports provided by Xmars to make informed decisions about your campaigns.

Trust the AI:

    Allow Xmars to automate repetitive tasks, but monitor its performance to ensure alignment with your goals.

Combine with Manual Oversight:

    While Xmars automates most tasks, occasional manual adjustments can further refine your campaigns.

Why Xmars AI is a Game-Changer

Xmars AI brings unparalleled precision, efficiency, and insights to Amazon ad campaigns. By automating time-consuming tasks like bid adjustments, keyword discovery, and performance monitoring, it allows authors to focus on growing their brand and creating new content. Its intelligent algorithms ensure your campaigns stay competitive, relevant, and profitable—making it an indispensable tool for authors aiming to maximize their impact on Amazon.

Xmars AI as Your Marketing Ally

Xmars AI takes the complexity out of managing Amazon ad campaigns by providing data-driven insights, automation, and optimization tools. Whether you're a new author or an experienced marketer, this tool can help you maximize visibility, drive sales, and improve ROI. By integrating Xmars into your advertising strategy, you can focus on what you do best—creating great books.

Use this link for a better offer from Xmars :

https://ai.xmars.com/register?version=lead&type=3&ref=tony41

Amazon Promotions

Amazon Promotions offers two primary avenues for authors to captivate new readers: Countdown Deals and Free Promotions. Each of these tools serves a unique purpose, letting authors strategically engage potential readers while encouraging them to dive into your literary work and inviting them into your narrative world. Let's explore how each of these promotional strategies functions and how you can leverage them to increase readership and sales.

Run a Price Promotion

Start a Kindle Countdown Deal or a Free Book Promotion. Note: Only KDP Select books are eligible. Only one promotion can be used per enrollment period.

- ⦿ Kindle Countdown Deals
- ○ Free Book Promotion

Create a Kindle Countdown Deal

Countdown Deals

Countdown Deals allow authors to temporarily discount their book prices while preserving the book's original royalty rate. This setup not only encourages impulse buying but also leads to increased downloads, given the sense of urgency and exclusivity created by the time-limited offer. Additionally, this promotion fuels a spike in visibility, propelling your book to rank higher in bestseller lists due to the increased sales volume during the deal period.

Key Steps for Implementing Countdown Deals:

1. Preparation: Ensure your book maintains a price above $2.99 to qualify for a Countdown Deal.
2. Timing: Schedule your deals strategically, aligning them with holidays, significant events, or concurrent promotions like book tours.
3. Promotion: Utilize social media, email newsletters, and book promotion platforms to maximize exposure during the discount period.

Countdown Deals not only boost immediate sales but also have a compounding effect on your book's overall ranking due to the sharp increase in velocity and downloads.

Step to create a countdown deal

1: Add books (only avaiable for Kindle Select enrolled books)

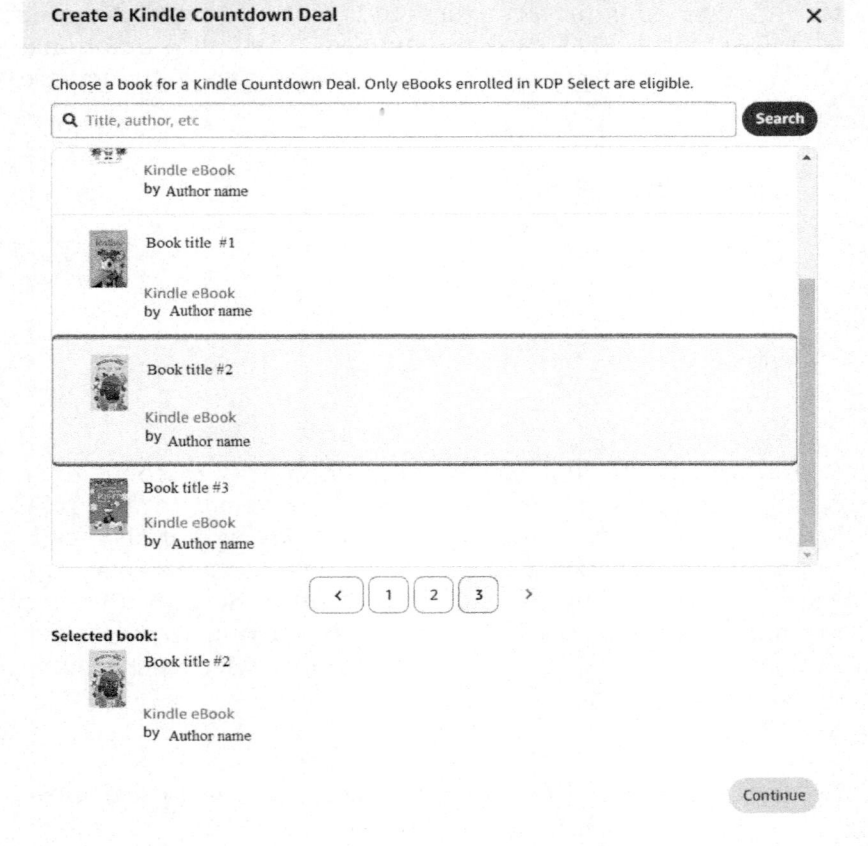

2. Then set up the countdown deal accordingly to your needs:

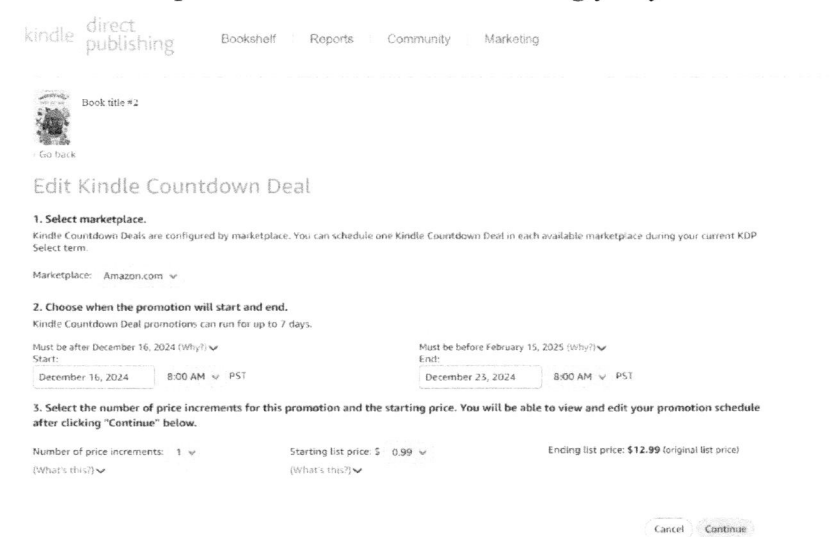

We will select the marketplace where the deal will take place, along with the start and end dates, as well as the price increments

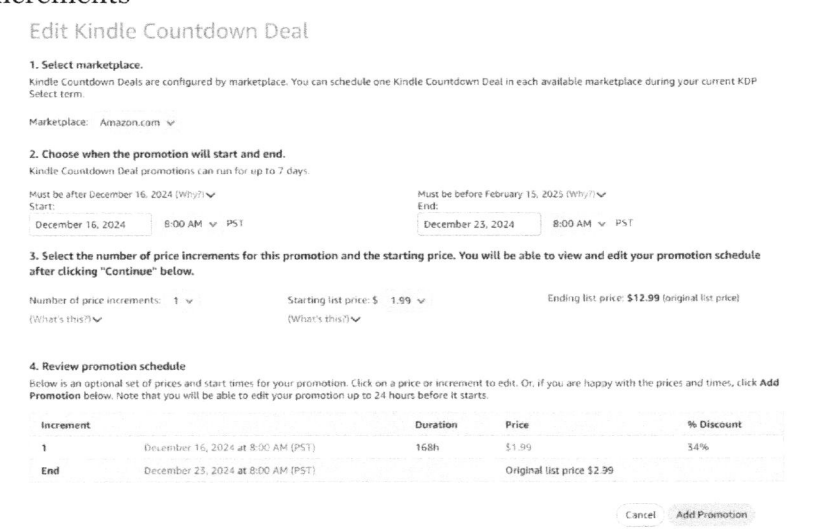

Click 'Continue' to preview the deal, and then select 'Add Promotion' if you are satisfied with the results.

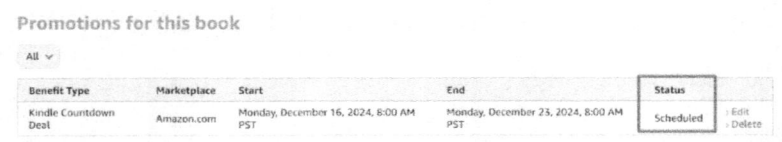

Promotions for this book

Benefit Type	Marketplace	Start	End	Status	
Kindle Countdown Deal	Amazon.com	Monday, December 16, 2024, 8:00 AM PST	Monday, December 23, 2024, 8:00 AM PST	Scheduled	Edit Delete

This will be the successfully scheduled for the promotion.

Free Promotions
Offering your book for free might seem counterintuitive, but it's a powerful tool for increasing downloads and visibility in your targeted audience's minds. Free promotions are excellent for drawing in undecided readers, providing them a risk-free opportunity to experience your content and potentially yield long-term fans who are willing to engage with future paid works.

Best Practices for Free Promotions:

1. Segmented Reach: Target niche audiences or groups who will benefit most from your book's message or theme.
2. Cross-Promotion: Collaborate with other authors or influencers to exalt mutual interest, exponentially broadening your promotional reach.
3. Callbacks: Employ captivating excerpts or cliffhangers within your book to propel readers toward intrigue for sequels or associated works.

Step to create a free book promotion
1. After choosing the free book promotion, add books
2. The setting here is simpler, we only need to choose dates

Book title #2

‹ Go back

Edit Free Book Deal

Choose when the promotion starts and ends. Start and end dates are midnight Pacific Time. For example, if you enter a start date of January 3 and an end date of January 7, your deal would run on January 3, 4, 5, 6, and 7.

Kindle Free Book Deal promotions can run for up to 5 days.

Start Date: November 28, 2024   End Date: November 30, 2024

Free promotion days used: 3 / 5

Cancel   Save Changes

We can run this free book promotion up to 5 days a time. And we're able to run this promotion every 90 days.
This will be the successfully scheduled for the promotion.

By leveraging Countdown Deals and Free Promotions systematically, authors can witness a synergic increase in book downloads, leading to higher royalties and expanded readership.

Section 2: Leveraging Social Media for Book Promotion

Social media is one of the most powerful tools for authors to connect with readers, build an audience, and drive book sales. Platforms like TikTok, YouTube, Instagram, and X (formerly Twitter) enable you to promote your book creatively, reach a global audience, and establish a strong author brand.

1. Choosing the Right Social Media Platforms

Not every platform will be ideal for every author. Your choice should depend on your target audience and book genre.

- TikTok (BookTok)

- **Why Use It:**

  TikTok is one of the fastest-growing platforms, with a thriving community of book lovers under the hashtag #BookTok.

  Great for fiction, young adult, and trendy self-help books.

- **Content Ideas:**

  Short videos of unboxing your book.

  Before-and-after shots of your cover design process.

  A day-in-the-life of an author video.

  Create challenges or trends tied to your book.

- **Pro Tip:** Use trending sounds and hashtags like #BookTok, #BooksOfTikTok, and #ReadingCommunity to boost visibility.

- YouTube

- **Why Use It:**

  ☐ Ideal for long-form content and in-depth discussions.

  ☐ Great for non-fiction authors who can provide tutorials, reviews, or expert advice related to their book.

- **Content Ideas:**

  ☐ Tutorials or lessons related to your book's subject.

  ☐ Author Q&A sessions or live streams.

  ☐ Book trailers showcasing your book with dramatic music and visuals.

- **Pro Tip:** Optimize your video titles with keywords (e.g., *"How I Wrote a Bestselling Self-Help Book"*).

- Instagram

- **Why Use It:**

  ☐ A visual platform perfect for showcasing book covers, quotes, and behind-the-scenes moments.

  ☐ Great for engaging with a creative and professional audience.

- **Content Ideas:**

  ☐ Post aesthetic images of your book paired with motivational quotes.

  ☐ Use Instagram Stories for polls (e.g., "Which cover design do you prefer?").

  ☐ Share snippets of your writing process.

- **Pro Tip:** Use hashtags like #Bookstagram, #AuthorsOfInstagram, and #IndieAuthor to reach book lovers.

- **X (formerly Twitter)**
  - **Why Use It:**
    Excellent for connecting with other authors, industry experts, and readers in real-time.

    Best for sharing quick updates, opinions, and engaging in discussions.
  - **Content Ideas:**
    Share short, engaging quotes from your book.

    Announce milestones (e.g., "We hit 100 reviews today!").

    Use threads to tell a compelling story related to your book.
  - **Pro Tip:** Participate in weekly hashtags like #WriterWednesday and #FollowFriday to grow your network.

2. Automating Social Media Content Creation

Creating consistent content can be time-consuming, but AI tools can streamline the process and keep your audience engaged.

Recommended AI Tools for Social Media:

- Pictory.ai:

    ☐ Generate video snippets from your book's content or blog posts.

    ☐ Add captions and visuals automatically.

- Canva:

    ☐ Create visually appealing posts, stories, and book teasers.

    ☐ Use pre-designed templates to save time.

- ChatGPT or Writesonic:

    ☐ Generate captions, hashtags, or content ideas for your posts.

Content Scheduling Tools:

- **Buffer or Hootsuite:** Schedule posts across platforms in advance.
- **Later:** Specifically optimized for Instagram and TikTok.

3. Engaging with Your Audience

Social media isn't just for broadcasting—it's for building relationships with your readers.

- Respond to Comments and Messages:

- Acknowledge your audience's questions, compliments, and feedback.

- Host Giveaways:

- Offer free copies of your book in exchange for likes, shares, or reviews.

- Example: *"Share this post for a chance to win a signed copy of my new book!"*

- Collaborate with Influencers and Readers:

- Partner with book bloggers or influencers to review your book.

- Feature user-generated content (e.g., photos of readers with your book).

- Measuring Success on Social Media

Use analytics tools to understand which strategies are working and where improvements are needed.

Key Metrics to Track:

- Engagement Rate:

- Measure likes, comments, and shares to determine how well your content resonates.

- Follower Growth:

- Monitor how quickly your audience is growing on each platform.

- Website Clicks:

- Track the number of users clicking on your Amazon link or website.

Tools for Analytics:

- TikTok Analytics (built-in for business accounts).
- Instagram Insights.

- Google Analytics for tracking traffic from social media to your website.

5. Real-Life Example: Promoting a Fiction Book on Social Media

Scenario:
An author launched a young adult fantasy book titled *"The Enchanted Chronicles."*

Steps Taken:

- TikTok Campaign:

☐ Created videos showcasing the magical illustrations in the book.

☐ Used the hashtag #BookTokFantasy, generating 50,000 views in one week.

- Instagram Stories:

☐ Ran a poll asking followers to guess the book's central mystery.

☐ Shared aesthetic photos of the book in enchanting settings.

- YouTube Trailer:

☐ Uploaded a cinematic book trailer highlighting the protagonist's journey.

Result: The author gained 10,000 followers across platforms and saw a 40% increase in Amazon sales during the launch month.

6. Common Social Media Mistakes to Avoid

Being Inconsistent:

 Post regularly to keep your audience engaged.

Ignoring Analytics:

 Failing to track metrics can result in wasted efforts on underperforming strategies.

Over-Promoting:

 Balance promotional content with engaging, value-driven posts.

Turning Social Media into a Sales Engine

Social media offers endless opportunities for authors to connect with readers, showcase their work, and drive sales. By choosing the right platforms, leveraging AI tools, and engaging authentically with your audience, you can create a powerful online presence that boosts your book's visibility and builds a loyal fan base.

The Power of Shorts: How Short-Form Videos Drive Viral Book Promotion on Amazon

Short-form video content has revolutionized the way products, including books, are marketed. Platforms like TikTok, Instagram Reels, and YouTube Shorts have emerged as powerful tools for creating viral moments, building communities, and driving book sales on Amazon.

Here's how short-form videos work and why they are essential for promoting your book.

1. Why Short-Form Videos Work

- Attention Economy

- Short videos (15–60 seconds) cater to today's short attention spans.
- They deliver a concise, engaging message that captivates viewers instantly.

- High Engagement Rates

- Platforms like TikTok and Instagram Reels prioritize short videos in their algorithms, giving them greater reach and visibility.
- Videos with engaging visuals, music, and storytelling can quickly attract thousands or even millions of views.

- Shareability

- Short videos are easy to share across platforms, allowing content to go viral organically.
- A single viral video can generate massive exposure for your book in a matter of hours.

2. Strategies for Using Shorts to Promote Your Book

- Create Teasers and Trailers

- Showcase the most exciting aspects of your book in a visually appealing way.
- Use dramatic music, text overlays, and compelling visuals to hook your audience.

Example:

- For a romance novel: Highlight a key emotional moment with captions like *"Will they end up together?"*

- For a self-help book: Use a motivational quote from your book paired with inspiring visuals.

- Leverage Trends and Challenges

- Stay updated on trending sounds, hashtags, and challenges on TikTok and Instagram.

- Incorporate these trends into your videos to increase visibility.

Example:

- If a popular TikTok sound is about making life changes, create a video showing how your self-help book provides actionable steps for transformation.

- Showcase the Creative Process

- Share behind-the-scenes glimpses of your writing, editing, or publishing journey.

- Use time-lapse videos to show how your book cover was designed or how you outline chapters.

Example:

- *"This is how I created the cover for my bestselling fantasy novel."*

- Highlight Reader Reactions

- Ask readers to share their reactions or reviews of your book in short videos.

- Feature user-generated content (UGC) to build social proof and community engagement.

Example:

- A reader might film a video saying, *"I couldn't put this book down—it changed how I think about mindfulness!"*

- Make It Relatable

- Tap into universal emotions or relatable scenarios that tie into your book's theme.

- Use humor, inspiration, or nostalgia to connect with viewers.

Example:

- For a productivity journal: A video showing someone overwhelmed by tasks followed by a clip of them organizing their day with your journal.

- Promote a Call-to-Action (CTA)

- Always include a clear CTA directing viewers to buy your book on Amazon.

- Use captions or visuals like *"Available now on Amazon"* with a clickable link in your profile.

3. Tools and Tips for Creating Effective Shorts

- AI Tools for Video Creation

- **Pictory.ai:** Converts text (like book excerpts) into engaging video snippets with visuals and captions.
- **Canva:** Offers pre-designed templates for TikTok, Instagram Reels, and YouTube Shorts.
- **CapCut:** A user-friendly editing tool for adding effects, music, and transitions.

- Tips for Success

Keep It Short and Sweet:
 Aim for videos between 15–30 seconds to hold attention.

Use Text Overlays:
 Add captions to ensure your message is understood even without sound.

Incorporate Strong Visuals:
 Use high-quality images or clips related to your book.

Hook Viewers in the First 3 Seconds:
 Start with an intriguing question, bold statement, or eye-catching clip.

Post Regularly:
 Consistency is key to building an audience and maintaining algorithmic visibility.

4. Real-Life Success Stories of Viral Book Promotions with Shorts

- Colleen Hoover's Novels on TikTok

•	Colleen Hoover's books gained massive popularity thanks to TikTok videos under #BookTok.

•	Short videos featuring emotional excerpts or reader reactions drove her books to the top of Amazon's bestseller charts.

- DIY Journals by Indie Creators

•	Independent authors have used Instagram Reels to showcase how their journals help with goal-setting, leading to thousands of sales.

•	Videos showing how to use the journal with time-lapse effects have gone viral.

- The Ripple Effect of Viral Shorts on Amazon Sales

Increased Traffic:

☐ Viral videos drive curious viewers to your Amazon page.

Higher Sales Velocity:

☐ A spike in sales improves your book's Amazon ranking, increasing its discoverability.

Social Proof:

☐ Viral content builds credibility, encouraging more readers to purchase.

- Common Mistakes to Avoid with Shorts

Overloading with Information:

Focus on one key message per video.

Ignoring Trends:

Failing to leverage current trends can limit your content's reach.

Low-Quality Visuals:

Poor lighting or grainy footage can reduce viewer engagement.

The Power of Shorts

Short-form videos are an invaluable tool for promoting your book on Amazon. By creating engaging, relatable, and visually compelling content, you can reach a global audience, generate buzz, and drive sales. Whether you're showcasing your book's highlights, connecting with trends, or sharing behind-the-scenes moments, leveraging the power of shorts can transform your book marketing strategy.

Success Case Study: Coco Wyo - From Amazon KDP to $10 Million a Year

Coco Wyo, a highly successful independent publisher on Amazon KDP, has built a $10 million-per-year passive income empire by combining the power of Amazon's self-publishing platform with an effective social media strategy, particularly leveraging YouTube Shorts. This case study explores how Coco Wyo achieved this milestone and offers actionable insights for replicating their success.

About Coco Wyo

Coco Wyo specializes in publishing low-content books, particularly coloring books for adults and children. Their books stand out due to:

- Unique and high-quality designs tailored to specific niches.
- A deep understanding of customer needs in the adult coloring book market, such as themes for stress relief, mindfulness, and creativity.

1. The Core of Their Strategy: Amazon KDP

- Focused Niche Selection

Coco Wyo dominates specific niches within the adult and children's coloring book market, such as:

- **Stress Relief Mandalas**
- **Fantasy and Mythical Creatures**
- **Seasonal Themes (e.g., Christmas, Halloween)**

Key Insights:

•   Instead of creating generic coloring books, Coco Wyo focuses on targeting niche audiences, ensuring lower competition and higher discoverability.

•   They use tools like **Publisher Rocket** and **Amazon search bar autocomplete** to identify keywords and themes with high demand.

- High-Quality Content

Coco Wyo invests in professional designs and illustrations that resonate with their target audience.

•   Each book features intricate and aesthetically pleasing designs.

•   They hire talented illustrators and use tools like **Canva** and **Adobe Illustrator** for professional-grade output.

- Leveraging Amazon SEO

Coco Wyo's books are consistently optimized for Amazon's search algorithm:

•   **Keyword-Rich Titles:** Example: *"Stress Relief Mandalas: A Mindfulness Coloring Book for Adults."*

•   **Backend Keywords:** Fully utilized to capture related searches.

•   **Visually Appealing Covers:** High-quality, trend-driven covers that attract attention.

- Scaling Through Volume

- Coco Wyo continuously publishes new books to target different sub-niches.

- With hundreds of titles available, they maximize their visibility and diversify their revenue streams.

2. Social Media Strategy: The Role of YouTube Shorts

Coco Wyo didn't just rely on Amazon's ecosystem; they turned to **YouTube Shorts** to amplify their reach and drive traffic to their books.

2.1. Why YouTube Shorts?

- YouTube Shorts offers global exposure, with billions of views daily.

- Unlike traditional YouTube videos, Shorts are quick to produce and optimized for virality due to their short runtime (15–60 seconds).

- How Coco Wyo Used YouTube Shorts

Showcasing Coloring Pages in Action:

☐ Coco Wyo creates Shorts featuring people coloring pages from their books.

☐ They highlight intricate designs being brought to life with vibrant colors, appealing to viewers' emotions and creativity.

Content Themes:

- **Relaxation and Stress Relief:** Videos showing slow, soothing coloring processes set to calming music.
- **Creative Challenges:** Encouraging viewers to complete a page and share their results.
- **Trending Themes:** Leveraging seasonal or trending topics, such as "Halloween Coloring Fun" during October.

Call-to-Action:

- Every video includes a clear CTA: *"Love this page? Get the full book on Amazon—link in description!"*

- Metrics of Success

- **Engagement:**

  Shorts often generate thousands to millions of views, building awareness and driving organic traffic to their Amazon listings.

- **Conversion Rates:**

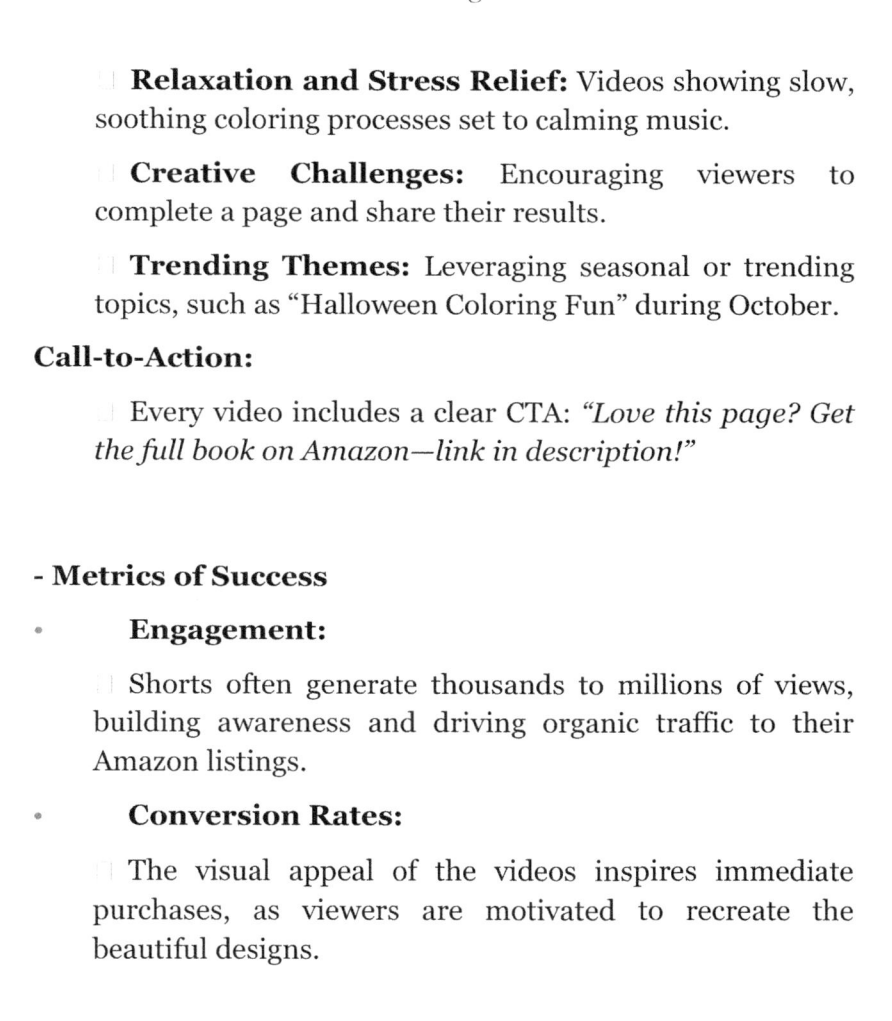

  The visual appeal of the videos inspires immediate purchases, as viewers are motivated to recreate the beautiful designs.

- Leveraging Other Social Media Platforms

Coco Wyo complements their YouTube Shorts strategy with Instagram Reels and TikTok.

- Instagram: Shares short clips and still images showcasing completed pages.

- TikTok: Engages with the creative community through challenges and trends.

3. Revenue Growth and Scale

- Estimated Revenue

- With multiple books consistently ranking in Amazon's bestseller lists for their categories, Coco Wyo generates revenue across hundreds of titles.
- The viral success of YouTube Shorts drives traffic and boosts sales, contributing to their $10 million annual income.

- Passive Income Model

- Once a book is published, it continues to generate sales without ongoing inventory costs or significant upkeep, thanks to Amazon's print-on-demand model.

4. Lessons from Coco Wyo's Success

- Target a Specific Niche:

- Narrow niches like "stress relief coloring books for adults" have dedicated audiences with high conversion potential.

- Invest in Quality:

- Coco Wyo's professional designs and polished presentation create lasting impressions and encourage repeat customers.

- Use Social Media to Amplify Visibility:

- YouTube Shorts and other short-form platforms drive massive traffic to their Amazon listings by showcasing the value of their books in action.

- Leverage SEO and Amazon Ads:

- Keyword optimization ensures that books rank high in search results.

- Sponsored Product Ads further boost discoverability during new launches.

- Scale Through Volume:

- Publishing multiple titles spreads risk, increases exposure, and ensures steady revenue streams.

5. How You Can Apply Coco Wyo's Strategy

Choose a High-Demand Niche:

Research niche opportunities using tools like Publisher Rocket or Amazon's autocomplete.

Focus on Quality:

Hire professional designers or use AI tools like **Leonardo AI** for illustrations.

Leverage YouTube Shorts and Social Media:

Create visually engaging videos showcasing your book's content.

Use trending sounds, hashtags, and challenges to increase reach.

Optimize for Amazon SEO:

Include niche-specific keywords in your title, subtitle, and metadata.

Scale Your Offerings:

☐ Publish multiple books to target different sub-niches and grow your catalog.

Conclusion: From Creativity to Profitability

Coco Wyo's journey from publishing low-content books to earning $10 million per year demonstrates the incredible potential of combining Amazon KDP with social media. By focusing on quality, leveraging trends, and consistently engaging with their audience, they've built a sustainable, scalable passive income model that inspires thousands of authors worldwide.

Would you like to explore this further or compile this into a document? Let me know!

User-Generated Content (UGC) to Build Social Proof and Community Engagement

User-Generated Content (UGC) is a powerful tool for authors to build trust, foster community engagement, and boost book sales. UGC involves content created by your readers, such as photos, videos, reviews, or social media posts that showcase their experience with your book.

Why UGC is Important for Book Marketing

- Social Proof:

Seeing other readers enjoy your book builds credibility and encourages potential buyers to make a purchase.

Reviews, photos, or videos from real readers act as endorsements for your book.

- Community Engagement:

Featuring UGC makes readers feel valued and encourages them to stay engaged with your brand.

This sense of connection can lead to repeat purchases and word-of-mouth referrals.

- Cost-Effective Marketing:

UGC is free content that promotes your book without requiring professional production.

Types of UGC for Book Promotion

- Photos:

Readers sharing pictures of your book in their personal spaces (e.g., on their bookshelf, desk, or nightstand).

- Videos:

TikTok or Instagram videos of readers unboxing your book or flipping through its pages.

Time-lapse videos of readers coloring in designs (for coloring books) or completing a journal entry.

- Reviews and Testimonials:

☐ Positive feedback shared as text, screenshots, or video testimonials.

☐ Snippets from Amazon or Goodreads reviews.

- Creative Submissions:

☐ Artwork inspired by your book or completed coloring pages from your coloring book.

☐ Book-inspired writing, such as poems or stories.

How to Encourage UGC

- Run Contests or Challenges:

☐ Offer prizes for readers who share creative content featuring your book.

☐ Example: *"Post a photo of your completed coloring page with the hashtag #MyCocoWyo for a chance to win a free book!"*

- Engage with Your Audience:

☐ Reply to comments, share posts, and thank readers for featuring your book.

- Incentivize Participation:

☐ Offer a discount code, free printable pages, or other bonuses for sharing UGC.

- Use Hashtags:

☐ Create a branded hashtag to make it easy for readers to share and discover related content.

☐ Example: #ReadersLove[YourBook] or #MyColorfulCocoWyo.

Showcasing UGC

- Social Media:

Repost UGC on your Instagram Stories, TikTok, or YouTube channel.

Add captions like *"We love seeing how [reader name] brought this design to life!"*

- Amazon Author Page:

Highlight positive reader reviews or UGC submissions in your book description.

- Newsletters:

Include UGC in your email updates to readers, showcasing their creativity.

- Website:

Dedicate a section of your website to feature reader submissions and reviews.

Case Study: Coco Wyo's Use of UGC

Coco Wyo successfully leveraged UGC to grow their brand and community:

- Encouraging Submissions:

Ran social media challenges like *"Show us your completed coloring pages!"*

- Sharing Reader Content:

Frequently reposted reader submissions on Instagram and TikTok, building a strong sense of community.

- Impact:

UGC increased engagement and strengthened customer loyalty, contributing to their $10 million annual revenue.

Pro Tip: Automate UGC Collection

Use tools like:

- **Later** or **Hootsuite:** Schedule and repost UGC automatically.

- **Hashtag Monitoring Tools:** Track branded hashtags to find new submissions.

Harnessing the Power of UGC

Featuring UGC is a win-win strategy—it boosts your book's credibility while strengthening your bond with readers. By encouraging and showcasing UGC, you can create a vibrant community around your book, amplify your marketing efforts, and drive more sales.

Section 3: Building an Email List of Readers

Email marketing remains one of the most powerful tools for connecting with your audience, promoting your book, and driving consistent sales. Unlike social media platforms, where algorithms dictate visibility, email provides a direct line to your readers. By building an engaged email list, you can create a loyal community of readers eager to support your work.

1. Why Build an Email List?

Direct Access to Your Audience:

Emails land directly in readers' inboxes, ensuring your message reaches them without competing with social media noise.

Longevity and Ownership:

Unlike social media followers, your email list is an asset you own. Algorithms won't limit your reach.

High ROI:

Studies show that email marketing generates $36 for every $1 spent, making it one of the most effective marketing tools.

Personalized Engagement:

Emails allow you to tailor messages to your readers' preferences and interests, creating a more intimate connection.

2. How to Build an Email List

Offer a Lead Magnet

A lead magnet is a free resource you offer in exchange for readers' email addresses.

Examples of Effective Lead Magnets:

- **Sample Chapters:**

    ☐ Provide the first chapter of your book for free.

    ☐ Example: *"Get a sneak peek of my new fantasy novel—download the first chapter for free!"*

- **Printable Worksheets:**

    ☐ For journals or self-help books, offer templates or guided prompts.

    ☐ Example: *"Download 5 free journaling pages from my bestselling mindfulness journal."*

- **Exclusive Designs:**

    ☐ For coloring books, offer downloadable pages.

    ☐ Example: *"Enjoy two free coloring pages from my new book!"*

- **Reader's Guide:**

    ☐ Create a discussion guide or companion resource for book clubs.

Create a Landing Page

Design a simple and compelling landing page where readers can sign up for your lead magnet.

What to Include:

- **Headline:**

Highlight the value: *"Unlock Your Free Bonus Content!"*

- Call-to-Action (CTA):

　　Use actionable language: *"Enter your email below to get your free download!"*

- Minimal Form Fields:

　　Request only essential information (e.g., name and email).

Tools to Use:

- **ConvertKit, Mailchimp, or GetResponse:** User-friendly platforms for creating landing pages and managing email lists.

Promote Your Lead Magnet

Drive traffic to your landing page through multiple channels.

Strategies:

- Social Media:

　　Post about your free resource on TikTok, Instagram, and X.

　　Example: *"Love adult coloring books? Download two free designs from my new release—link in bio!"*

- Amazon Author Page:

　　Include a link to your landing page in your author bio.

- Inside Your Book:

　　Add a CTA in your book encouraging readers to sign up for additional resources.

☐ Example: *"Want more coloring fun? Visit [website] for free pages and updates!"*

- Collaborations:

☐ Partner with other authors or influencers to promote each other's lead magnets.

3. Engaging Your Email List

Once readers subscribe, keep them engaged with consistent and valuable communication.

Welcome Email Sequence

Create an automated series of emails to welcome new subscribers.

Example 3-Email Sequence:

- Email 1:

☐ Thank them for signing up and deliver the promised lead magnet.

☐ *"Here's your free coloring pages—enjoy!"*

- Email 2:

☐ Share your story as an author and introduce your book.

☐ *"Why I wrote this journal—and how it can help you."*

- Email 3:

☐ Offer a limited-time discount or exclusive access to your book.

☐ *"Get 20% off my book for the next 48 hours!"*

Regular Newsletters

Send periodic emails to nurture your relationship with readers.

What to Include:

- Updates:

  Announce new books, projects, or events.

- Behind-the-Scenes Content:

  Share insights into your writing process or upcoming plans.

- Exclusive Offers:

  Provide discounts or special deals to your subscribers.

- Valuable Content:

  Offer tips, stories, or resources related to your book's theme.

  Example: *"5 mindfulness tips to reduce stress—straight from my journal!"*

Use AI for Automation and Personalization

AI tools can help you save time and improve engagement by personalizing emails.

Recommended Tools:

- Mailchimp or ConvertKit:

  Automate email campaigns and segment your audience based on preferences.

- Writesonic or ChatGPT:

  Generate compelling email content tailored to your audience.

4. Measuring Success

Track key metrics to understand your email marketing performance and make improvements.

Important Metrics:

- Open Rate:

☐ The percentage of subscribers who open your emails. Aim for 20–30%.

- Click-Through Rate (CTR):

☐ The percentage of readers who click on links within your emails.

- Unsubscribe Rate:

☐ Monitor this to ensure your content remains relevant and engaging.

Tools for Analytics:

• Most email marketing platforms include built-in analytics dashboards.

5. Real-Life Example: Building an Email List for a Coloring Book

Scenario:

An author published an adult coloring book focused on stress relief and used email marketing to build a loyal audience.

Steps Taken:

- Lead Magnet:

☐ Offered two free printable coloring pages in exchange for email sign-ups.

- Promotion:

Shared the lead magnet on Instagram and inside the book's introduction.

- Engagement:

Sent bi-weekly newsletters featuring completed reader designs, stress-relief tips, and book updates.

Result:

- Built an email list of 10,000 subscribers in six months.
- Used email campaigns to drive a 30% increase in sales during book launches.

6. Common Mistakes to Avoid

Sending Too Many Emails:

Avoid overwhelming subscribers—stick to a consistent but reasonable schedule.

Focusing Only on Promotions:

Balance promotional content with value-driven emails to keep readers engaged.

Neglecting Mobile Optimization:

Ensure emails are easy to read on mobile devices.

Turn Subscribers into Loyal Fans

Building an email list is one of the most effective ways to cultivate a community of loyal readers. By offering valuable resources, engaging authentically, and leveraging automation tools, you can create a direct marketing channel that drives book sales and fosters long-term relationships with your audience.

Section 4: Collaborating with Book Promotion Sites

Book promotion sites can be a game-changer for authors looking to increase visibility, drive downloads, and boost sales. These platforms cater to book lovers who are actively seeking new reads, making them a prime audience for your work. By leveraging book promotion sites, you can amplify your marketing efforts and reach a larger, more targeted audience.

1. Why Use Book Promotion Sites?

Access to Targeted Readers:

☐ These platforms attract avid readers who are already searching for books in specific genres or niches.

Boost Sales and Rankings:

☐ Promotions can lead to a surge in downloads and sales, improving your book's visibility on Amazon.

Cost-Effective Marketing:

☐ Many sites offer affordable packages that provide significant exposure compared to other marketing channels.

Credibility and Trust:

☐ Being featured on a reputable book promotion site adds credibility to your book and boosts trust among potential buyers.

2. Top Book Promotion Sites

Here's a list of some of the most popular and effective book promotion sites to consider:

- BookBub:

    Known as the gold standard for book promotions.

    Offers targeted campaigns based on readers' preferences.

    Cost: Higher than most, but delivers high ROI.

- Bargain Booksy:

    Focuses on promoting discounted books.

    Ideal for price promotions, such as $0.99 or free eBooks.

- Freebooksy:

    Promotes free eBooks to a large audience.

    Excellent for building your email list or boosting downloads.

- Fussy Librarian:

    Offers personalized recommendations to readers.

    Low-cost options for authors.

- ManyBooks:

    Targets both free and discounted books.

    Broad audience reach with affordable pricing.

- EReader News Today:

    Specializes in promoting Kindle eBooks.

    Works well for Amazon-focused campaigns.

- Book Gorilla:

　　☐ Delivers daily email recommendations to readers.

　　☐ Focused on both free and discounted books.

3. How to Collaborate with Book Promotion Sites

Step 1: Research and Choose the Right Site

•　　Identify the sites that align with your book's genre and goals.

•　　For example:

　　☐ Use **BookBub** for high-impact campaigns targeting a broad audience.

　　☐ Use **Freebooksy** for free eBook promotions.

Step 2: Prepare Your Book for Promotion

- Optimize Your Listing:

　　☐ Ensure your book has a professional cover, compelling description, and high-quality formatting.

- Offer Discounts:

　　☐ Most promotion sites work best with discounted or free books.

　　☐ Example: Lower your Kindle eBook price to $0.99 for the duration of the promotion.

- Accumulate Reviews:

　　☐ Having a good number of positive reviews increases the likelihood of acceptance by premium sites like BookBub.

Step 3: Submit Your Book

Follow each site's submission guidelines carefully.

Be prepared to provide:

Book cover image.

Genre and category.

Book description.

Promotion dates and pricing.

Step 4: Plan the Timing

- Schedule promotions around new releases, seasonal themes, or major sales events (e.g., Black Friday).

4. Maximizing Results from Book Promotions

Combine Promotions with Other Marketing Efforts:

- Pair your book promotion site campaign with Amazon Ads or social media campaigns for maximum impact.

Promote Across Platforms:

- Announce the promotion on your email list and social media to drive additional traffic.

Leverage Free Downloads for Long-Term Gains:

- Free downloads can help you:
  - Increase reviews.
  - Gain visibility in Amazon's "Also Bought" section.

Analyze Results:

- Track key metrics like downloads, sales, and ranking improvements.
- Use this data to refine future campaigns.

5. Real-Life Example: Using BookBub for a Self-Help eBook

Scenario:
An author published a self-help book titled *"Breaking Free: Overcoming Anxiety and Stress."*

Steps Taken:

- Promotion Plan:

- Lowered the book's price to $0.99 for a one-week promotion.
- Scheduled a BookBub campaign targeting readers interested in mental health and self-help.

- Results:

- Achieved over 10,000 downloads during the promotion.
- Increased Amazon sales rank, leading to sustained sales post-promotion.

6. Common Mistakes to Avoid

Choosing the Wrong Site:

- Not all sites are suitable for every genre or book type. Research is crucial.

Poorly Timed Promotions:

Avoid scheduling promotions when your audience may not be actively buying (e.g., off-season periods).

Skipping Book Optimization:

A lack of reviews or an unprofessional cover can hinder your promotion's success.

Elevate Your Reach with Book Promotion Sites

Collaborating with book promotion sites is a highly effective way to amplify your book's visibility and sales. By choosing the right platforms, preparing your book for success, and integrating promotions with other marketing efforts, you can achieve significant results and build momentum for your publishing journey.

Section 5: Analyzing and Iterating for Success

Marketing isn't a one-time effort; it's an ongoing process of learning, improving, and scaling your strategies. To ensure your book marketing efforts deliver the best results, analyzing key performance metrics and iterating based on insights is essential. This section focuses on how to measure success, identify areas for improvement, and refine your marketing strategies for long-term growth.

1. Why Analysis and Iteration Are Critical

Understand What Works:

Data helps you identify which strategies drive the most sales, clicks, or downloads.

Optimize ROI:

☐ By focusing resources on high-performing campaigns, you can maximize your return on investment.

Adapt to Changing Trends:

☐ Reader preferences and market trends evolve. Regular analysis ensures you stay relevant.

Build a Scalable Framework:

☐ Iteration allows you to refine your processes, creating a repeatable system for future book launches.

2. Tools for Tracking Performance

Amazon KDP Dashboard

- **Key Metrics:**

  ☐ Sales and royalties.

  ☐ Page reads (for Kindle Unlimited).

  ☐ Geographical sales data.

Book Promotion Platforms

- Sites like BookBub and Freebooksy provide performance insights for campaigns, such as:

  ☐ Number of downloads.

  Engagement rates.

Analytics Tools

Google Analytics: Track traffic and conversions from external sources like email campaigns or social media ads.

Mailchimp or ConvertKit: Monitor email open rates, click-through rates, and subscriber growth.

Ad Platforms
Amazon Ads Dashboard:

Click-through rate (CTR).

Advertising cost of sales (ACOS).

Conversion rates.

Social Media Ad Platforms (e.g., Facebook Ads):

Impressions, engagement, and conversion metrics.

3. Key Metrics to Monitor
Sales Metrics:

Daily and monthly sales volume.

Total revenue generated.

Traffic Metrics:

Number of visitors to your Amazon book page or author website.

Sources of traffic (e.g., email, social media, ads).

Engagement Metrics:

Reviews and ratings on Amazon and Goodreads.

Social media comments, shares, and likes.

Ad Performance Metrics:

CTR: Measures how effective your ads are at driving clicks.

ACOS: The percentage of ad spend relative to sales. Aim for a balanced ACOS based on your profit margins.

4. Strategies for Iteration

Refine Amazon SEO

Use performance data to update your book's keywords, title, and description.

Replace underperforming keywords with high-traffic alternatives identified through tools like Publisher Rocket or BookBeam.

Adjust Pricing Strategies

Test different price points to find the sweet spot for your audience.

Example: Offer temporary discounts during key promotional periods to boost sales.

Optimize Ad Campaigns

Pause or lower bids on underperforming keywords.

Allocate more budget to high-converting campaigns.

Use AI tools like Xmars for automated bid adjustments and keyword analysis.

Experiment with New Channels

Try promoting your book on additional platforms like TikTok or Pinterest if your target audience is active there.

Collaborate with influencers or bloggers to reach untapped markets.

Real-Life Example: Iterating on a Children's Storybook Campaign

Scenario: An author launched a children's bedtime storybook and used Amazon Ads, a BookBub campaign, and social media to promote it.

Initial Results:

The Amazon Ads campaign had a high CTR but low conversion rates.

The BookBub campaign drove significant downloads but few reviews.

Actions Taken:

Analyzed Ad Performance:

> Found that broad match keywords were attracting irrelevant clicks.
>
> Switched to exact match and phrase match keywords like "bedtime stories for toddlers."

Incentivized Reviews:

> Followed up with BookBub readers via email, offering a bonus story in exchange for an honest review.

Refined Targeting:

> Used audience insights to target parents on Instagram with video ads.

Outcome:

Increased conversion rates by 25%.

Earned 50 new reviews in two weeks.

Sales doubled after optimizing campaigns and leveraging reader feedback.

Common Mistakes to Avoid

Neglecting Data:

Failing to analyze results can lead to wasted marketing spend.

Overreacting to Short-Term Results:

Give campaigns enough time to collect meaningful data before making drastic changes.

Ignoring Reader Feedback:

Reviews often highlight areas for improvement, such as unclear formatting or misleading descriptions.

Building a Sustainable Framework

Schedule Regular Reviews:

Analyze performance weekly or monthly to stay on top of trends.

Document Lessons Learned:

Keep a record of what works and what doesn't to inform future campaigns.

Scale Successful Strategies:

Allocate more resources to the channels, platforms, or tactics that deliver the best results.

Data-Driven Growth

Analyzing and iterating on your marketing efforts is the key to long-term success as an author. By using data to refine your strategies, you can maximize sales, minimize wasted effort, and build a scalable framework for future book launches. Remember, the more you learn from your efforts, the more effective and efficient your marketing will become.

Chapter 5: Scaling Your Business and Diversifying Income

This chapter is focused on helping authors transition from occasional book publishing to building a sustainable and scalable publishing business. It covers strategies to expand your catalog, leverage multiple platforms, build a personal brand, and diversify income streams for long-term financial success.

Section 1: Expanding Your Catalog Strategically

Expanding your book catalog is one of the most effective ways to grow your publishing business and increase revenue. A well-planned catalog not only attracts new readers but also retains existing ones, encouraging repeat purchases. In this section, we'll explore the strategies for scaling your catalog with purpose and efficiency.

1. The Power of a Series

Why a Series Works

Readers who enjoy the first book in a series are highly likely to buy subsequent installments.

A series builds anticipation and loyalty, keeping readers engaged with your brand.

Promoting a series is easier, as the success of one book often drives sales of others.

Examples of Successful Series

Fiction:

A mystery series where each book explores a new case but features the same detective.

A fantasy trilogy with interconnected story arcs.

Non-Fiction:

A self-help series covering different aspects of personal growth, such as productivity, mindfulness, and relationships.

How to Plan a Series

For Fiction:

Develop a central theme or character that ties the series together.

Use cliffhangers or unresolved subplots to encourage readers to continue.

For Non-Fiction:

Divide a broad topic into smaller, actionable themes.

Example: A fitness series could include books on diet plans, workout routines, and mental health tips.

2. Targeting Evergreen Niches

Why Evergreen Niches Matter

Evergreen niches have consistent demand, ensuring long-term sales.

Examples include:

- Self-help topics like productivity and mindfulness.
- Low-content books such as planners, coloring books, and journals.
- Children's books with universal themes like friendship and kindness.

Steps to Identify Evergreen Niches

Research Amazon's Best Sellers and trending categories.

Use tools like Publisher Rocket to analyze keyword demand and competition.

Consider niches with a wide audience appeal and lasting relevance.

3. Scaling Through Volume

Why Volume Matters

Publishing more books increases your visibility on Amazon, giving readers more opportunities to discover your work.

A diverse catalog allows you to experiment with different niches and styles.

How to Scale Effectively

Leverage AI Tools:

- Use ChatGPT to generate outlines, drafts, or ideas for content books.
- Use Canva or MidJourney to create professional-quality covers and illustrations.

Repurpose Content:

Adapt a single book idea into multiple formats or niches.

Example: Turn a self-help book into a companion journal or workbook.

Set a Consistent Publishing Schedule:

Aim to release books regularly to maintain momentum.

Plan seasonal releases for topics like holiday-themed coloring books or journals.

Real-Life Example: Scaling a Catalog with Purpose

Scenario:
An author started with a single mindfulness journal and scaled to a robust catalog of over 30 books.

Steps Taken:

Expanded into related niches, such as gratitude journals and goal planners.

Created a mindfulness book series, with titles like *"Mindfulness for Beginners"* and *"Mindfulness for Busy Professionals."*

Used AI tools for quick drafting and design, cutting production time by 50%.

Result:

Increased monthly sales from $500 to $5,000 within a year.

Gained a loyal audience eager for new releases.

Expanding your catalog strategically is the cornerstone of building a scalable publishing business. Whether through a well-planned series, targeting evergreen niches, or leveraging AI for efficiency, the key is consistency and quality. A robust catalog not only increases revenue but also positions you as an authority in your chosen genres.

Section 2: Selling Books on Multiple Platforms

To grow your publishing business beyond Amazon KDP, it's essential to explore additional platforms and formats. Selling your books across multiple platforms not only diversifies your income streams but also increases your reach and establishes your presence in new markets.

1. Beyond Amazon KDP

While Amazon KDP is a fantastic starting point, there are other platforms that can complement your publishing efforts and reach a wider audience.

IngramSpark

What It Offers:

- Print-on-demand (POD) services for physical books.
- Distribution to bookstores, libraries, and global markets.

Key Advantages:

- Your book can appear in physical retail stores like Barnes & Noble.
- Offers both hardcover and paperback options.

How to Get Started:

Upload your book files (formatted to IngramSpark's specifications).

Set distribution preferences, pricing, and royalty percentages.

Barnes & Noble Press

What It Offers:

Self-publishing platform for eBooks and print books.

Access to the Barnes & Noble marketplace.

Key Advantages:

Ideal for authors targeting U.S.-based readers.

Marketing tools to increase visibility within the Barnes & Noble ecosystem.

How to Use It:

Set up an account and upload your book files.

Use promotional tools to reach Barnes & Noble customers.

2. Create Audiobooks

Why Audiobooks Are Essential

The audiobook market has grown exponentially, with millions of readers opting for audio over traditional formats.

Creating an audiobook allows you to tap into this lucrative market and reach listeners who prefer consuming content on-the-go.

Platforms for Audiobooks

ACX (Audiobook Creation Exchange):

Amazon's platform for creating and distributing audiobooks.

Distributes to Audible, Amazon, and iTunes.

Findaway Voices:

Distributes to a wide range of retailers and libraries globally.

Offers flexible pricing and narration options.

How to Create Audiobooks

Hire a Narrator:

Use ACX to connect with professional narrators or voice actors.

Choose a narrator who matches your book's tone and audience.

Experiment with AI Narration:

For smaller budgets, consider AI voice tools like **Speechify** or **Murf.ai** to create cost-effective audiobooks.

Promote Your Audiobooks:

Highlight the audiobook version in your marketing campaigns.

Bundle eBook and audiobook discounts to encourage cross-format purchases.

3. Diversify Through Direct Sales

Selling books directly to readers allows you to retain more profits and build a closer relationship with your audience.

Setting Up a Personal Website

Use platforms like **WordPress**, **Wix**, or **Shopify** to create an author website.

Features to Include:

- A storefront for selling books directly.
- Lead capture forms to build your email list.
- Blog content to attract organic traffic.

Benefits of Direct Sales

Higher Profit Margins:

Avoid platform fees and retain full control over pricing.

Customer Data:

Access email addresses and demographics to enhance future marketing efforts.

Brand Building:

Establish your brand identity beyond Amazon or other retailers.

Real-Life Example:

An indie author set up a Shopify store and offered exclusive signed copies of their books. By marketing the exclusivity, they earned an additional $2,000 per month from direct sales.

Conclusion

Selling books on multiple platforms is a strategic way to diversify your income streams and expand your audience. Whether it's reaching global readers through IngramSpark, tapping into the audiobook market with ACX, or building your brand through direct sales, each channel adds value to your publishing business. By leveraging these opportunities, you can create a sustainable and scalable framework for long-term success.

Section 3: Building a Personal Brand as an Author

In the crowded publishing industry, building a personal brand is essential for standing out and creating a loyal reader base. A strong personal brand not only attracts readers but also establishes your credibility, fosters trust, and opens opportunities for collaborations and diversified income streams.

1. Establishing Your Presence

Why Your Personal Brand Matters

A recognizable brand helps readers connect with you on a deeper level, increasing their loyalty and willingness to support your work.

It creates a sense of professionalism, encouraging partnerships with influencers, publishers, and other authors.

Steps to Establish Your Presence

Define Your Brand Identity:

Determine the tone, style, and values that resonate with your audience.

Example: If you write self-help books, your brand might focus on inspiration, empathy, and actionable advice.

Create Consistent Branding:

Use the same colors, fonts, and logo across all platforms (website, social media, book covers).

Develop a tagline or slogan that encapsulates your mission, such as *"Inspiring Growth Through Mindfulness."*

Launch a Professional Website:

Use platforms like WordPress or Wix to create an author site.

Essential elements:

- About page with your author story.
- A catalog of your books with links to purchase.
- A blog or resources section to share valuable content.

2. Engaging with Your Community

Build a Connection with Readers

Host Interactive Sessions:

Live Q&A sessions on Instagram or YouTube to discuss your writing process, upcoming releases, or themes from your books.

Respond to Comments and Messages:

Make readers feel appreciated by acknowledging their support.

Create Exclusive Content:

Share behind-the-scenes content, deleted scenes, or early drafts to make readers feel involved in your creative journey.

Examples of Community Engagement

Social Media Challenges:

Example: *"Complete this page from my new coloring book and share it using #MyColorfulJourney!"*

Reader Spotlights:

Feature fan art, photos, or testimonials on your social media or website.

3. Monetizing Your Brand

Your personal brand can become a source of additional income when leveraged effectively.

Ideas for Monetization

Courses and Workshops:

Teach skills related to your book's content, such as *"How to Self-Publish Your First Book"* or *"The Art of Journaling for Stress Relief."*

Sponsorships and Collaborations:

Partner with brands or businesses that align with your niche.

Example: Collaborate with a stationery company if you publish planners or journals.

Merchandising:

Sell branded products like mugs, T-shirts, or bookmarks featuring designs or quotes from your books.

Paid Memberships or Subscriptions:

Offer exclusive content through platforms like Patreon or Substack.

Perks could include early book releases, private Q&A sessions, or personalized advice.

Real-Life Example: An Author Who Built a Personal Brand

Scenario:

A non-fiction author focused on productivity built a brand around the theme of *"Mastering Your Day."*

Steps Taken:

Launched a YouTube channel with weekly videos sharing productivity tips.

Created an Instagram page featuring motivational quotes from their book.

Hosted live workshops on time management techniques.

Results:

Gained 50,000 Instagram followers in a year.

Increased book sales by 40% through consistent social media engagement.

Generated an additional $20,000 annually from workshops and online courses.

4. Tools for Building Your Brand

Social Media Management Tools:

> Use Buffer or Hootsuite to schedule posts and manage multiple platforms.

Design Tools:

> Canva for creating branded graphics and visuals.
>
> Tailor Brands for logo and branding kit creation.

Email Marketing Platforms:

> ConvertKit or Mailchimp to nurture your audience with newsletters and updates.

Building a personal brand as an author is about creating a lasting impression that resonates with your readers. By establishing a strong presence, engaging authentically, and leveraging monetization opportunities, you can transform your writing career into a sustainable business. A well-crafted brand doesn't just sell books—it creates a loyal community that supports you for years to come.

Section 4: Creating a Passive Income Ecosystem

A sustainable publishing business goes beyond just book sales. By diversifying your income streams and leveraging your intellectual property creatively, you can build a robust passive income ecosystem. This section explores strategies to generate revenue through licensing, affiliate marketing, memberships, and more.

1. Licensing and Intellectual Property

Licensing your content opens the door to additional income streams by allowing others to use your work in different formats and markets.

Types of Licensing Opportunities

Educational Materials:

Adapt your content for schools, workshops, or corporate training programs.

Example: A self-help book could be licensed as a course module for employee development.

Translations and International Rights:

License your book for translation into other languages to reach global audiences.

Work with foreign publishers or platforms like Babelcube.

Film and TV Adaptations:

Fiction books, especially those with strong narratives, can be adapted into movies or series.

Example: Pitch your story to production companies or scriptwriters for consideration.

2. Affiliate Marketing

Affiliate marketing allows you to earn commissions by promoting products or services related to your book's content.

How It Works

Add affiliate links to your website, blog, or email newsletters.

Recommend tools and platforms you use, such as:

>**Publisher Rocket** for keyword research.
>
>**Canva Pro** for designing book covers or marketing materials.

Examples of Affiliate Opportunities
Amazon Affiliate Program:

>Earn commissions on sales generated through affiliate links to your book or related products.

Specialized Programs:

>Join affiliate programs for niche-specific tools or services.
>
>Example: A fitness author could promote workout equipment or apps.

3. Memberships and Subscriptions

Membership platforms like Patreon or Substack provide a recurring income model by offering exclusive content or experiences to your most dedicated fans.

What to Offer

Exclusive Content:

> Early access to new books or chapters.
>
> Behind-the-scenes updates on your writing process.

Personalized Experiences:

> Live Q&A sessions or one-on-one coaching.
>
> Signed copies of books or custom dedications.

Bonus Resources:

> Printable journals, templates, or additional book content.
>
> Example: *"Bonus workbook for my bestselling self-help guide."*

How to Get Started

Choose a platform:

> **Patreon** for a tiered membership system.
>
> **Substack** for subscription-based newsletters.

Promote your membership program on social media and within your books.

4. Merchandising

Branded merchandise not only generates additional revenue but also strengthens your personal brand.

Popular Merchandise Ideas

Custom Merchandise:

> Mugs, T-shirts, and tote bags featuring quotes or designs from your book.

Book-Related Items:

> Bookmarks, journals, or coloring supplies (if you sell coloring books).

How to Sell Merchandise

Use platforms like **Teespring** or **Printify** for on-demand printing and shipping.

List your merchandise on your author website or link to it from social media.

5. Real-Life Example: A Passive Income Success Story

Scenario: An author who published a series of productivity books created a passive income ecosystem that earned $100,000 annually.

Steps Taken:

Licensed the series to a corporate training company for employee workshops.

Joined affiliate programs for tools like Evernote and Trello, earning commissions from referrals.

Launched a Patreon membership with tiers offering exclusive webinars and signed books.

Created branded merchandise, including planners and motivational posters.

Result:

Diversified income sources provided stability and reduced reliance on book sales alone.

The brand became synonymous with productivity, opening doors to speaking engagements and partnerships.

6. Common Mistakes to Avoid

Overcomplicating Your Ecosystem:

Start with one or two additional revenue streams and expand gradually.

Neglecting Your Core Audience:

Ensure that new ventures align with your readers' interests and needs.

Low-Quality Products or Services:

Maintain the same high standards for all your offerings to protect your brand reputation.

Creating a passive income ecosystem allows you to maximize the value of your intellectual property and build a sustainable publishing business. Whether through licensing, affiliate marketing, memberships, or merchandising, these strategies enable you to earn consistently while expanding your brand's reach. A well-planned ecosystem not only provides financial stability but also frees you to focus on what you do best—writing.

Section 5: Final Case Study and Call to Action

To illustrate the principles discussed throughout this book, this section highlights a comprehensive case study of an author who successfully scaled their KDP publishing business into a thriving brand. It concludes with actionable steps to inspire you to take the first step toward your own publishing success.

Case Study: From First Book to Multi-Platform Publishing Success

Background

An aspiring author started with a single self-help book titled *"Small Steps, Big Changes"* aimed at helping readers build better habits. With no prior experience in publishing, the author relied on Amazon KDP and strategically integrated AI tools, social media, and passive income strategies to grow their brand.

Phase 1: Launching the First Book

Research and Preparation:

> Used **Publisher Rocket** to identify high-demand, low-competition keywords such as "daily habits," "self-improvement," and "habit tracker."

> Designed a professional cover using **Canva Pro** and created a compelling book description.

Marketing Strategies:

> Ran a free promotion using **Freebooksy** to gain initial downloads and reviews.

> Promoted the book through Instagram Reels and TikTok videos, focusing on relatable content like *"5 Habits That Changed My Life."*

Results:

> Gained 2,000 downloads during the first week.

Received 50+ reviews within a month, boosting the book's visibility on Amazon.

Phase 2: Expanding the Catalog

Creating a Series:

Released follow-up titles like *"Small Steps for Big Productivity"* and *"Small Steps for Big Mindfulness."*

Used AI tools like **ChatGPT** to draft outlines and generate engaging content.

Targeting Evergreen Niches:

Launched companion products such as a *"Big Changes Journal"* and a *"Daily Habit Tracker"* to complement the original book.

Leveraging New Formats:

Produced audiobooks for each title using **ACX**, tapping into the growing audiobook market.

Phase 3: Scaling Across Platforms

Multi-Platform Presence:

Published physical copies through **IngramSpark** to reach bookstores and libraries.

Listed the books on **Barnes & Noble Press** to target U.S.-based readers.

Building a Personal Brand:

Created a YouTube channel sharing productivity tips and excerpts from the books.

- Grew an email list of 20,000 subscribers by offering free habit-tracking templates.

Generating Passive Income:

- Earned affiliate commissions by promoting habit-tracking apps and productivity tools on their website.
- Launched a Patreon membership offering exclusive webinars and habit-building challenges.

Results

Monthly revenue grew from $500 in the first month to $10,000 within the first year.

The author transitioned into a full-time publishing career with a diversified income ecosystem.

The brand became a recognized name in the self-help niche, opening opportunities for speaking engagements and sponsorships.

Call to Action: Your Turn to Build a Publishing Empire

This book has equipped you with the tools, strategies, and inspiration to start and scale your Amazon KDP publishing business. Whether you're creating your first book or expanding an existing catalog, success is within your reach if you take consistent, purposeful action.

Actionable Next Steps

Define Your Niche:

Use tools like **Publisher Rocket** or **Google Trends** to identify profitable niches.

Leverage AI Tools:

Streamline content creation with **ChatGPT**, design stunning covers with **Canva**, and generate visuals using **MidJourney**.

Build Your Marketing Strategy:

Utilize Amazon Ads, social media platforms, and book promotion sites to maximize visibility.

Expand and Diversify:

Plan a series, explore new formats like audiobooks, and build a personal brand to create additional income streams.

Start Now:

The best time to begin your journey is today. Take small steps every day, and you'll build your publishing empire over time.

Conclusion: A Journey Towards Success

You have just completed an incredible journey—one that has taken you from understanding the Amazon KDP platform, exploring the power of artificial intelligence (AI), to planning and building your very own publishing empire. But this is not the end; it's the beginning of a new adventure—one where you will write your own story of success.

The Power of Small Ideas

Every book, whether a lengthy masterpiece or a simple low-content creation like a journal, begins with an idea. The difference between a mere idea and monumental success lies in action. Now, you have the knowledge, tools, and strategies—everything you need to make it happen.

Remember, those who succeed on Amazon KDP are not necessarily the most talented, but they are the ones who take consistent action and continuously improve. Your first book may not be perfect, but it is the vital first step on a path filled with possibilities and inspiration.

Challenges Are the Seeds of Growth

No one achieves success without encountering challenges. You might face days with low sales, ad campaigns that don't perform well, or reviews that don't meet your expectations. But it's within these challenges that you'll learn, grow stronger, and create results that surpass your dreams.

Always remember: every small step has value. Every word you write, every ad you launch, every connection you build with readers—it all contributes to the foundation of your success.

Passion Is the Guiding Light

Keep the fire of your passion burning bright. Every book you create is not just a product but a piece of your soul, a part of your story shared with the world. Readers can feel the authenticity and dedication in every page, and that's why they will keep coming back to you.

The world will always need storytellers, educators, and those who bring value. You have the opportunity to be one of them—so turn that opportunity into reality.

The Future Is in Your Hands

This book is not just a resource—it's an invitation. You don't need to have all the answers right now. All you need is a decision—to begin. Each book you publish is a chance to change your life and the lives of others.

Take the leap, embrace the risks, and trust that every step you take brings you closer to your goals. Remember, the most successful people aren't those who never make mistakes, but those who never give up.

Your Story Is Just Beginning

Success is not a destination; it's a journey. Don't be afraid to start small. One book. One idea. One action. That's all it takes to begin writing your own success story.

The world is waiting for what you create. Your books will touch hearts, change lives, and leave a lasting impact. Don't keep your story to yourself—start today and show the world the power you bring.

The future is in your hands—write your own story.

If you ever need support or more inspiration, remember that you are not alone. This book, along with all the tools and the community you build, will always be by your side on this journey.

Start. Act. Shine.

Q&A: Frequently Asked Questions About This Book

Q1: Who is this book for?

This book is for anyone who wants to create a sustainable online income and achieve financial freedom through Amazon KDP and AI tools. Whether you're:

A beginner with no prior experience in publishing.

An entrepreneur looking to diversify income streams.

A creative individual passionate about sharing stories or ideas.

Someone seeking freedom from the 9-to-5 grind.

If you want to turn your ideas into passive income and design a flexible lifestyle, this book is for you.

Q2: Do I need any prior experience to succeed with Amazon KDP?

No prior experience is required! This book is designed to guide you step by step, from understanding Amazon KDP to creating and marketing your books effectively. With the help of AI tools, even beginners can produce professional-quality content and achieve success.

Q3: What types of books can I publish on Amazon KDP?

Amazon KDP supports a wide range of book types, including:

Fiction: Novels, short stories, fantasy, romance, thrillers, and more.

Non-Fiction: Self-help, business, personal development, cookbooks, and more.

Low-Content Books: Journals, planners, coloring books, logbooks, and sketchbooks.

Children's Books: Picture books, early readers, and educational material.

Specialty Books: Niche-focused titles, such as hobby guides or travel diaries.

Q4: How much money can I realistically make with Amazon KDP?

The income potential with Amazon KDP varies based on factors like the quality of your books, niche selection, marketing efforts, and consistency. Some authors make a few hundred dollars a month, while others earn thousands or even millions annually. This book provides strategies to help you maximize your earning potential and scale your business.

Q5: How does AI help in the publishing process?

AI tools are game-changers in self-publishing. Here's how they can help:

Content Creation: Use AI tools like ChatGPT to generate ideas, draft content, and edit text.

Design: Platforms like Canva and MidJourney make creating professional book covers and illustrations easy.

Marketing: AI-powered platforms like Xmars can optimize ad campaigns and track performance to increase your book's visibility.

With AI, you save time, reduce costs, and produce high-quality results without needing advanced technical skills.

Q6: What are the most important steps to success on Amazon KDP?

The most critical steps include:

Finding the Right Niche: Use tools like Publisher Rocket and BookBeam to identify profitable, low-competition niches.

Creating High-Quality Content: Leverage AI tools and professional design platforms to produce polished, engaging books.

Optimizing Amazon SEO: Craft keyword-rich titles, descriptions, and categories to rank higher in Amazon search results.

Marketing Effectively: Utilize Amazon Ads, social media platforms, and book promotion sites to reach your audience.

Building a Brand: Expand your catalog, engage with readers, and establish a recognizable author presence.

Q7: How long does it take to create and publish a book?

The timeline depends on the type of book and the tools you use. With AI assistance:

Low-content books (e.g., journals, coloring books): 1–2 weeks.

Non-fiction guides or storybooks: 1–2 months.

Fiction novels or detailed projects: 3–6 months or longer, depending on complexity.

This book provides tips to streamline your workflow and speed up production without compromising quality.

Q8: What are the costs involved in starting with Amazon KDP?

Amazon KDP is a low-cost business model with minimal upfront expenses. Some potential costs include:

Book Production: Free if using AI tools or DIY; optional costs for hiring designers or editors.

Marketing: Budget for Amazon Ads, promotions, and social media campaigns.

Tools and Subscriptions: Platforms like Canva Pro, Publisher Rocket, or AI tools may require a subscription.

This book also outlines free and budget-friendly alternatives to help you get started with minimal investment.

Q9: Can I publish books if I'm not a good writer?

Absolutely! With AI tools like ChatGPT, you don't need to be a professional writer to create compelling content. These tools can help you generate ideas, structure your book, and polish your language. Additionally, this book shares strategies for outsourcing tasks like design or editing if you prefer to focus on other aspects of your business.

Q10: How do I scale my publishing business?

Scaling involves expanding your catalog, diversifying your income streams, and leveraging multiple platforms. Strategies covered in this book include:

Publishing a series to keep readers engaged.

Selling your books on platforms like IngramSpark and Audible.

Building a personal brand to attract loyal readers.

Creating passive income through licensing, affiliate marketing, and merchandise.

Q11: What challenges should I expect, and how can I overcome them?

Challenges may include:

Low Sales Initially: Focus on marketing and Amazon SEO to increase visibility.

Competition: Target niche markets with less competition and high demand.

Learning Curve: This book simplifies the learning process and provides actionable steps to guide you.

Remember, persistence and consistency are key. Learn from setbacks and adapt your strategies to overcome obstacles.

Q12: What's the first step I should take after reading this book?

Start by defining your niche and brainstorming book ideas. Use the tools and strategies outlined in this book to validate your ideas, create a plan, and take action. Remember, the journey to success begins with that first step.

Tony Trieu

Printed in Great Britain
by Amazon